Copyright © 2016 by Lani Sharp
All rights reserved. This book or any portion thereof
may not be reproduced or used in any manner whatsoever
without the express written permission of the publisher
except for the use of brief quotations in a book review.

Printed in Australia

First Printing, 2016

ISBN 978-0-9945052-0-0

White Light Publishing House
6 Lincoln Way
Melton West, VIC, Australia 3337

www.whitelightpublishingau.com

☙ DEDICATION ❧

This book is wholly dedicated to my stepdad Barry, the most inspiring Libran in my Universe, without whom this whole book series may not have been possible. Tragically, after a short illness, Barry departed from this world in February 2016, around the time of the series' release date. With a heavy heart but the most beautiful of memories – particularly of your zest for life, hearty laugh, sincere warmth, enthusiasm, and larger than life hopes and dreams – I thank you for your love, encouragement, support, understanding, advice, inspiration, friendship, belief in me, and for being such a wonderful part of my journey. Everything you have ever done for me is so very appreciated. You may have departed this earthly experience, but you will never leave my heart or my thoughts. I sincerely promise that I will fulfil the dreams that you didn't get the chance to. Never forgotten.

26 September 1950 – 18 February 2016

"Now flying with the cosmic angels."

ABOUT THE AUTHOR

☾ ★ ☽

Lani Sharp is a Natural Born Rebel who just also happens to be an Aquarian, who shunned 'conventional' astrology courses to pursue her own path in the wondrous, inspiring and ever-evolving field of cosmic forces and stellar influences. After failing to find a course or tutor that suited her needs, Lani set out on her own starry Magic Carpet adventure across the skies, partly to discover her own 'truths' about this ancient system, but mostly to prove that one can achieve absolutely anything, including and above all, their dream careers (or lifestyle), if they put their hearts and souls into it. A self-taught astrologer who takes the esoteric and spiritual approach to this much-loved popular art, she has been studying and effectively practising astrology since she was eight years old. When she is not writing about, channelling, practising or teaching astrology, she can be found living her dream life alternating somewhere between her home in Australia's stunning Tropical North or her second home in Victoria's beautiful Dandenong Ranges, enjoying tea parties with her highly imaginative Cancerian daughter, Allira, and their gnome and fairy friends, crystal-wishing, day-dreaming, believing in gnomes, pixies, angels, fairies, magic and miracles, honing her magickal * witchcraft skills, Moon-gazing, Sun-worshipping, Venus-channelling, Jupiter-drawing, assisting others to discover, unravel and follow their true spiritual paths … or of course walking across rainbows!

Not a mistake. Magick is a Wiccan variation of the word 'magic'.

★

ACKNOWLEDGEMENTS, CREDITS & GRATITUDE BLESSINGS

☆

I would love to thank the following people and entities for their amazing contributions, interest, support and faith in me as I wrote the manuscripts for each of the twelve astrological Sun signs. Firstly, the biggest thank you go to my Mum, Sandra, and my stepdad, Barry, for their unending support, love, advice, daily Skype conversations, acceptance of our geographical distance, and above all, their inner knowing that everything always comes together in the end. Your support of me and my dreams is appreciated beyond words. Secondly, gratitude to my wonderful partner, Travis, for his patience (no mean feat for a Gemini!), for supporting me every step of the way, and for his acceptance of my 'mad scientist' Aquarian mindset by never trying to break down the invisible 'laboratory' walls I built around myself while writing the books. I would also like to extend my enormous gratitude to the following: Allira, my little Cancerian 'crab' daughter, a soul in a billion, who also had to tolerate and operate within the bounds of her nutty professor mother's antics and focus throughout the writing of the books. Thank you to Nicola, my wonderful Facebook friend, for recommending White Light Publishing House, and of course to White Light Publishing House themselves, for pouring their faith and passion into my project from the very beginning - and an even bigger thank you to the wonderful people behind the company for publishing my work, Christie and Jess! Gratitude also goes out to my dear friends, both near and far, who have inspired in me so many ideas through simply being themselves - especially Amanda and Carlie. Amanda, you have always been my 'astrology buddy' and I have always enjoyed - and learned so much through - our discussions on all things astrology and star signs: the good, the bad and the ugly! Having someone like you off which to bounce thoughts and share ideas with, has always been immensely helpful and appreciated. I have saved my final thank you for The Universe, who always delivers to me exactly what I have asked for, without exception. The Universe is my ultimate *higher power*, my guiding light, my powerful driving force, my spiritual helper, my guardian angel, my eternal friend, my inner motivator, my sympathetic listener, my inspirational teacher, and the fulfiller of all my dreams, including this one, having my very first book(s) published, a long-held dream that stretches way back through the years to my days of being a mini dreamer, inquisitor and stargazer. The Universe has always believed in me, but perhaps more importantly, I have always believed in *IT*.

So to all of the above, I wish to say:

Thank you, thank you, thank you!

"We were born at a given moment, in a given place, and like vintage years of wine, we have the qualities of the year and of the season in which we are born"

Carl G. Jung

"There was a star danced,
and under that I was born"

William Shakespeare

INSPIRED BY ALL THE SIGNS

Aries imparted courage and boldness
And helped me dance away the pain
Taurus gave me hugs and comfort
And shelter from the rain
Gemini provided me with laughter
And taught me again how to have fun
Cancer nurtured and sustained me
By reflecting back my Sun
Leo reminded me there was joy
From within myself and above
Virgo awakened my healthy glow
By teaching me how to love
Libra gave me gentle hugs
And judged me not for a thing
Scorpio lent me some of his power
And took away the sting
Sagittarius showered me with gifts
Of words so wise and true
As Capricorn led the way up the mountain
My resolve and strength grew
Aquarius gave me the gift of friendship
And carried me as his brother
And Pisces swam with me to the depths
With a compassion like no other.

Special Note

Throughout the text of this book, and indeed the whole Lucky Astrology book series, I have capitalised the first letter of the word 'Universe'. This is because, quite simply, I feel it is a very special title for the higher power that I personally choose to be guided by, and have accordingly highlighted it as such.

You may also notice that I use the words 'he' or 'she', and 'his' or 'her', when referring to your own Sun sign and other zodiac signs, and never 'he or she' or 'his or her' together. The reason for this is for simplicity, for I don't wish the sentences to be too wordy and therefore the messages within them to be lost. As a general rule, I refer to all six 'masculine' zodiac signs as 'he', and all six 'feminine' signs as 'she', and this remains a consistent rule throughout this book and the whole series.

Your Sun sign, Libra, is a masculine sign and will thus be referred to accordingly.

CONTENTS

	Page
ASTROLOGY	15
THE ZODIAC & YOUR PLACE IN THE SUN	24
LIBRA THE SCALES	31
QUOTES BY LIBRANS	37
THE LIBRA CONSTELLATION	42
THE LIBRA SYMBOL	44
THE RUNDOWN & LESSONS ★	
THE ESSENCE OF LIBRA	47
THE THREE DECANS OF LIBRA	60
YOUR ELEMENT ★ AIR	64
YOUR MODE ★ CARDINAL	86
YOUR RULING PLANET ★ VENUS	88
YOUR HOUSE IN THE HOROSCOPE ★	
THE SEVENTH HOUSE	101
YOUR OPPOSITE SIGN ★ ARIES	105
MAGIC, DRAWING, ATTRACTION, SPELLS,	
RITUALS, WISHING & POWER	115
ASTROLOGY & MAGIC	120
PLANETS ★ DAYS OF THE WEEK	
& THEIR POWERS	126
YOUR NATAL MOON PHASE	130
SPELLS, MAGIC & WISHING WITH MOON PHASES	133
THE MOON ★ WHAT T REPRESENTS IN THE	
HUMAN PSYCHE & NATAL CHART	140
YOUR MOON SIGN	143
YOUR BODY & HEALTH	152
THE CELL SALTS ★ ASTROLOGICAL TONICS	156

	Page
AIR SIGN LIBRA & THE SANGUINE HUMOUR	159
MONEY ATTRIBUTES	162
COLOURS ★ YOUR LUCKY COLOURS	165
LUCKY CAREER TIPS	177
LUCKY PLACES	181
GEMS & CRYSTALS	182
LIBRAN POWER CRYSTALS	195
YOUR LUCKY NUMBERS	204
YOUR LUCKY MAGIC HOURS OR TIME UNITS	212
YOUR LUCKY DAY ★ FRIDAY	217
YOUR LUCKY CHARM / TALISMANS	221
YOUR LUCKY ANIMALS & BIRDS	224
YOUR METALS	236
PLANTS, HERBS, SPICES, TREES, SHRUBS, FLOWERS, SCENTS & INCENSE	240
YOUR FOODS	245
YOUR LUCKY WOOD & CELTIC TREE ★ SYCAMORE & VINE OR IVY	247
THE POWER OF LOVE	254
LUCKY IN LOVE? LIBRA COMPATIBILITY	266
YOUR TAROT CARDS	283
LUCKY 13 TIPS	303
HAVE YOU PACKED YOUR MAGICAL BAG FOR THE JOURNEY?	306
A FINAL WORD ★ TAPPING INTO THE MAGIC OF LIBRA	307

LUCKY ASTROLOGY

By Lani Sharp

LIBRA

Tapping into the Powers of Your Sun Sign for Greater Luck, Happiness, Health, Abundance & Love

"That which is above is like to that which is below, and that which is below is like to that which is above, to accomplish the miracles of one thing … the Father thereof is the Sun, the mother the Moon."

The Emerald Tablet, Hermes Trismegistus (circa 3000 BC)

★ ASTROLOGY ★

Astrology: "Divination through the correlation of earthly events with celestial patterns"
'Real Magic', I. Bonewits, 1971

A BRIEF HISTORY

Astrology can be defined as the calculation and meaningful interpretation of the positions and motions of the heavenly bodies, and their correlation with human experiences. Its central concept is based upon this interconnectedness or correspondence between the stars and ourselves.

The word astrology is derived from the Greek word astron, meaning 'star' and logos which means 'word'. Astrology, therefore, literally means language of the stars. It is based on the ancient law known as 'As Above, So Below', otherwise known as the Law of the Macrocosm and Microcosm. The Macrocosm is the Universe, symbolised by the sky, the starry dome that we can see from the Earth; the Microcosm is us - humans, and all other life on Earth. 'As Above, So Below' is a well-known and deeply impressing maxim of Hermetic origin, inscribed upon the famed Emerald Tablet among cryptic wording by enigmatic figure, Hermes Trismegistus, around 5,000 years ago. These four powerful words are adopted by astrologers and believers in magic to explain, in very succinct wording, the meaning behind the art and science of celestial influences upon our Earthly affairs.

Astrology and many other magical and occult studies, propose that we are not separate from the Universe, we are part of it. The Sun, Moon and planets all follow exact patterns of movement and their motions can be measured precisely by astronomers. The basic idea of astrology is that all individual parts of the Universe, from plants to animals, cooperate with each other and work together in harmony.

Anyone can apply astrological knowledge in their daily lives, but it hasn't always been like that. At one time, astrology was reserved only for Kings and nations, and only the court astrologer/astronomer could cast and interpret horoscopes. Ancient astrology and astronomy used to be one and the same. To be an astrologer, you first had to be able to interpret the stars in some systematic way, and then track the movement of the Moon and the planets against the background of the constellations.

Astrology, the knowledge and language of the cosmos, goes back to the ancient kingdom of Babylonia and was adapted by the Mesopotamians, Greeks, Egyptians and Romans to incorporate their own deities (as indicated in mythology). It is upon a combination of Greek and Egyptian interpretations of astrology that our present knowledge is based.

In the ancient Mesopotamian world, as far back as 800 BC, people lived precariously beneath the open skies. The skies and the stars which filled them, were the real founders of astrology. Today we are aware that the Sun and Moon exert a profound influence upon our Earthly affairs, but for our primitive ancestors, the heavens, the stars and the planets must have been a matter of great and mysterious significance. Early humankind, its senses influenced by natural processes of ebbs, flows, growth, decay and cycles, tended naturally towards a physical explanation of the Universe. At first, the movements of the planets - and all celestial occurrences - were observed as omens affecting the Ruler and his nation; it was only in Egypt in the fifth century AD that the casting of horoscopes for individual people and the calculation of the planetary positions at the time of birth became widespread.

The first astrologers, the Chaldeans, mapped the stars and later passed this knowledge and wisdom on to the ancient Greeks, who, during the third century BC, developed astrology into a science with the use of mathematical aids and instruments to measure planetary movements. The Greeks were the first to cast individual horoscopes. And it was the Greeks who associated the four elements with the signs of the zodiac. The word "zodiac" can be translated from Greek to mean the "circle or path of the animals." The Greeks not only had names for the twelve Solar phases but had symbols for each, and many correspond with the ones we use today.

The Greeks passed on much of their knowledge to the Romans. During the second century BC, Roman astrologers were primarily forecasters who were consulted frequently by rulers of the church and state. By the early third century AD, astrology co-existed with early Christianity. This harmonious co-existence was possible because it was considered that celestial bodies could foretell events, but did not determine the future - indeed, the stars seen by the shepherds at the time of Christ's birth were only predictors of his arrival. After the fourth century AD, Christianity strengthened and the popularity of astrology declined as Christian reluctance to support 'pagan' or 'superstitious' beliefs became more prominent. The Middle Ages saw a revival in astrology, with courses being taught in universities and other educational establishments, and connections were made between the zodiac, alchemy, herbs and medicine. Astrology was once again able to exist alongside the Church, although many remained suspicious of astrologers.

Around the beginning of the fifteenth century, academics of the Renaissance movement examined the past for knowledge, and ancient philosophies, including astrology, flourished; this coincided with arts and science movements developing. The famous prophet and astrologer Nostradamus lived during this period. Leonardo da Vinci depicted aspects of astrology combined with geometry in his art. Writers and poets of the time, including Shakespeare, alluded to zodiacal influences in their work.

During this period, astrology had numerous practical applications. Agricultural calendars were introduced, indicating favourable planting times according to the phases of the Moon; health and illness were linked with movements of celestial bodies; and emotional states and mental health afflictions correlated with the planetary positions.

Eventually, new ways of thinking led to a split between astronomy and astrology, and by the seventeenth century, the realm of science had developed to such a degree that astrology was no longer taken seriously.

The study of the sky above us has been charted for more than 5,000 years. This fact is known because ancient 'horoscopes' imprinted on clay tablets have been unearthed, dating back almost 5,400 years ago. However, no one knows for certain just how, when and where astrology first began, although it is known that it flourished in ancient Chaldea, Mesopotamia, Babylon and Egypt.

Astrology is a science which has spanned many centuries and still remains extraordinarily popular, and its truths have the potential to speak to and *through* all of us. Long before today's interest in it, men of great vision such as Ptolemy, Hippocrates, Plato, Galileo, Jefferson, Franklin, Newton, Columbus and Jung respected its inherent truths, mythology and eternal knowledge. Furthermore, astrology predates many other 'sciences' - for out of it grew religion, medicine and astronomy, not the other way around.

The discipline of astrology is ultimately a study of the interlocking and interrelated forces of the twelve zodiacal forces, or constellations, that grace the heavens, as they pour their energies into the Earthly kingdoms below. As these various energies circulate throughout the etheric realm of our Solar system, these zodiacal entities and archetypes imprint their vibrational frequencies and harmonic resonances upon our bodies, minds, souls and spirits.

ASTROLOGY & THE INDIVIDUAL

Since the earliest period of the history of humankind, people studied the starry vaults of the heavens and conceived that their presence, movements and positions endowed planet Earth's inhabitants with Divine influence. There is much evidence that positions and movements of the planets as seen from Earth at the time of a birth are linked to personality characteristics of individuals. Human energy and emotional cycles are governed by the forces and networks of magnetic impulses from all the planets. Of all the heavenly bodies, the Moon's effects and power are the most marked and visible due to its close proximity to Earth. But the Sun, Venus, Mars, Mercury, Jupiter, Saturn, Uranus, Neptune and Pluto exercise their influences just as surely. In fact, scientists are aware that plants and animals are affected by natural cycles which are governed by forces such as fluctuations in barometric pressure, the gravitational field and electricity in the air. These Earthly dynamics are originally triggered by magnetic vibrations from the atmosphere, or outer space, from where the planets send forth their unseen waves. No living organism or mineral on Earth escapes these immense, if unseen, influences.

The geomagnetic field seems to affect life on Earth in certain observed ways, and these influences appear to correlate with planetary positions. It has been suggested that the fluctuations of the Earth's magnetic field are picked up by the nervous system of the in utero infant, which acts like an antenna, and these synchronise the internal biological clocks of the foetus which control the moment of birth. The foetal magnetic antenna therefore, is sensitive enough to sense these planetary vibrations and fields, and through a combination of inherited genetics and the positions of the planets at birth, they are imprinted with certain basic inherited and 'absorbed' personality characteristics.

Carl Jung, the Swiss psychiatrist and psychological theorist, suggested that the inherent disposition of the individual is present at birth, and is reflected in the patterns of his or her natal chart. Further, he theorised that there is a 'priori factor' in all human activities, namely the inborn, preconscious and unconscious individual structure of the psyche. The preconscious psyche, for example that of a newborn baby, is not simply an empty vessel into which practically anything can be poured, but rather it is this preconscious psyche that gives us the free will to become what we are instead of what others or our environment makes us. The child is not merely a receptacle for the psychic life of those around him or her, albeit sensitive and susceptible to the surrounding unconscious forces in childhood; for he/she also brings something of his own to his experience of them.

Further, Dr Harold S. Burr, who was a Professor of Anatomy at the Yale University School of Medicine, and author of *The Nature of Man and the Meaning of Existence* (1962), asserted that there is order in the Universe, unity in the organism and man is endowed with a soul. He stated that a complex magnetic field not only establishes the pattern of the human brain at birth, but continues to regulate and control it through life, and that the human central nervous system is a superb receptor of electro-magnetic energies, indeed the finest in nature. He contended that the electro-dynamic fields of all living things, which may be measured and mapped with standard voltmeters, mould and control each organism's development, health and mood, and named these fields 'fields of life'.

It can therefore be suggested that astrological and planetary influences endow us with the majority of our characteristics at birth, characteristics bestowed upon us according to our Sun sign and other planetary forces. Other parts of the chart are also highly significant and need to be integrated for a 'whole' picture to form, however the Sun sign is an excellent starting point.

The ancients taught that astrology was one of the keys to the many enigmas that plague humans in their unceasing quest to determine what the meaning of life is, and what their role and place in the Universe is - and this quest still persists today. Astrology, which dates back over 5,000 years, is indeed one such key to unlocking the many secrets of the Universe - and ultimately, the individual self.

"KNOW THYSELF"

"Man, know thyself.
All wisdom centres on this."
Carl Jung

Before the temple of the Oracle at Delphi, the ancient Greeks imparted a special piece of advice that was carved onto one of the portals: "Know Thyself." These two powerful words are easy enough to understand, but much more difficult to apply. Throughout life's inner and outer journey, astrology can provide us with an inner navigational system by which we can be guided towards our highest potential, and closer towards the eternal quest of 'knowing thyself'. It provides the hope that this higher spiritual plane exists and that if we can 'read' and therefore be guided by the unique inner blueprint that our individual birth chart has stamped upon us at the moment we take our very first breath, indeed we can reach this higher spiritual plane and realise our innate potential.

Always remember that astrology is not fatalistic. The stars may incline, but they do not compel. Astrology simply provides us with an inner guide, a blueprint, for our journey through life and the finding of our true selves - and what we do with the resulting knowledge is entirely up to us.

Good luck on your journey!

THE ZODIAC & YOUR PLACE IN THE SUN

The zodiac is a circle of 360 degrees, consisting of equal segments of 30 degrees each. These represent the twelve houses of the twelve astrological signs. This zodiac is how the early astrologers imagined the Solar system to be, a perfect circle with the Earth at its centre, around which the Sun, Moon and the planets revolved. Each sign of the zodiac corresponds to one of the twelve segments, following a chronological order and established according to the rhythm of the seasons and cycles of the Sun and the Moon. But the zodiac itself, or the band of constellations which comprise it, has shifted over the millennia, creating division between astronomical and astrological schools of thought. It has been said that due to this shift over time, one who once considered themselves as an Aquarian, is actually a Capricorn, the sign before it, and a Leo is actually a Cancerian, its preceding sign. This is the result of misunderstandings and differences in perspectives, and explanations around it are beyond the scope of this book, but can be researched further should you wish to delve a little deeper. From the astronomical point of view, it is true that the zodiac to which we refer today is not situated where it 'should' be, but indeed, nothing is fixed under the celestial vault. And so the starting point of the ancient zodiac does not correspond exactly to the one we can observe today. But for the purposes of increasing your power and luck, let's keep things simple and enjoy the ride; after all, astrology - while based upon many scientific theories, mysteries, scepticism, superstitions, facts, measurable patterns, ambiguities, correlations, paradoxes, contradictions, links, stigmatisms and observations that seek to support, refute, prove and disprove this ancient art time and again - is ultimately meant to be *fun* too!

THE SUN

Earth's Luminary ★ *Our Brightest Shining Star*

Our Centre, Core Self, Identity & Inner Guiding Light

"Perfect is what I have said of the work of the Sun."
Hermes Trismegistus, *The Emerald Tablet*

The Sun is our essence, centre, source, ego strength, power, life force, will, vitality, creative expression, purpose, life's direction, our sense of identity, and who we really *are*. Our brightest star is the core of our individuality, our inner guiding light. The Sun is externalising, and represents totality, infinity, eternity, the striving toward and ultimate reaching of one's personal destiny, and *completion* in all areas. It is the creative energising giver of life and the 'father' of the zodiac. It endows us with our inherent creative potential and personal identity - our urge to *create* and to *be*. The Sun is our core self, conscious purpose, our sense of creating something out of our own being. It is the integrated personality and represents the *present*, our greatest Gift. The Sun rules the heart and is thus symbolically the centre of self. Indeed, the Sun *is* the heart and the most commanding presence in our birth chart; the luminary Ruler who governs our essential self and wants to be noticed and appreciated, and above all, to *shine*.

★ KEY WORDS ★

Identity, core self, spirit, life force, power, essence, creativity, higher self, the Father, ego, vitality, pride, individuality, leadership, majesty, inner authority, will, expression, willpower, purpose, the journey, the path and the destiny.

THE SUN ★ THE ULTIMATE SOURCE OF LIFE ON EARTH

Throughout the ages, and indeed since life forms began, the electromagnetic waves generated by the Sun have kept planet Earth habitable for humans, animals, plants and minerals. The Sun is, in fact, the only true source of energy on planet Earth. It provides the perfect amount of energy for plants to synthesise all of the products required for growth and reproduction, which is then stored by plants and ingested by humans and animals who, through many complex processes, utilise these various forms of encapsulated Solar energy - and so the cycle continues. Wood, fuel and minerals (crystals included), too, are merely various forms of this encased Sun energy. In fact, all matter is essentially 'frozen' light. Human body cells are bundles of Sun energy; we couldn't conceive or process a single thought without the molecules of Solar-energised oxygen and glucose.

In essence, the Sun supports the growth of all species, including human beings and microscopic life forms, and without it life on Earth would simply not be possible. The mathematical and metaphysical complexity that stands behind a system of organisation and order so infinitely diverse and intricate as planetary life cannot be truly fathomed, but unerringly and miraculously, the Sun instinctively knows what each species, from a tree to a human, intrinsically needs in order to fulfil its evolutionary purpose and cycles.

Ultimately, the electromagnetic waves generated by the Sun come in a variety of lengths, which determine their specific course of action and responsibility. There are gamma rays, x-rays, cosmic rays, various kinds of ultraviolet rays, infrared, short-wave infrared, radio waves, electric waves, and of course the visible light spectrum, consisting of the seven colour rays.

Most of these energy waves are absorbed and used for various processes in the layers of atmosphere that encircle the Earth, and only a small portion of them - the electromagnetic spectrum - reach the surface of our planet. Although the human eye is only able to perceive about one percent of this spectrum, the waves exert a very strong influence upon us. The waves and rays which do affect us so profoundly, allow all life forms to undergo constant cycles of change necessary for growth and renewal. Physically, we can observe this, but on a deeper, more spiritual plane, we can even *feel* it and allow its radiance to permeate our very souls. Such is the might, force and power of that astonishing ball of fire in our sky: the brilliant, ever-shining Sun.

THE SUN ★ WHAT IT REPRESENTS IN THE HUMAN PSYCHE & NATAL CHART

✡

"The Sun is the most powerful of all the stellar bodies. It colours the personality so strongly that an amazingly accurate picture can be given of the individual who was born when it was exercising its power through the known and predicable influences of a certain astrological sign; these electromagnetic vibrations will continue to stamp that person with the characteristics of their Sun sign as they go through life."
Linda Goodman's Sun Signs, **Linda Goodman, Pan Books, 1968**

The Sun is our essence, our core self, conscious purpose and sense of identity, our creative potential, our spirit, the integrated personality that shines outward from within us. It is concerned with the present. It is our centre, source, power, life force, will, vitality, purpose, life's direction, what and who we *really* are.

The Sun represents our basic urge for self-expression. It is the 'Solar energy cell' in a person's character, the Lord and giver of life, and symbolises the way in which an individual will shine out to the world. Our Sun is our personal identity and aspects to it from other components in the chart show the ease or otherwise of assuredness and confidence with which one will project and express one's individuality. The Sun sign will also show how an individual bounces back from setbacks and disappointments, their resilience and their general outward expression of energy.

The Sun is the archetype of the Father and represents the primary masculine principle in the natal chart. It indicates how we express and experience our masculine side, or animus, our conscious self, how we express ourselves creatively, our personal potential, individuality, self-expression and personal power. It has to do with courage, power, generosity, creativity, vitality, self-confidence, nobility, self-worth, dignity and strength of will. It symbolises authority and purpose, the *ruler*, and its potential is the peak of constructive maturity. It signifies self-sufficiency and abundance, containing enough energy to radiate warmth and give life to everything around it.

The sign in which one's Sun is posited, and its placement in the birth chart, strongly indicates the level and type of vitality available to the personality (the sign), and in which area of life this may be most strongly directed (the house).

The Sun in a natal chart is a powerful symbol because everything is filtered, at a conscious level, through it. It tells us what we need to do to feel fully alive, the type of engine 'driving' us, what we need to do to be authentic and to be fully functioning. Listening to the special message of one's Sun sign can provide one with greater direction, and a more dynamic energy and life purpose.

The symbol for the Sun ☉ depicts a circle with a dot or 'seed' at its centre, from which the core self, power, creativity and the first sparks of life can spring. The circle around this 'seed' represents spirit, symbolising wholeness, eternity and the never-ending flow of energy.

While the Moon, the night sky's luminary, represents the *soul*, the Sun, the day sky's luminary, represents our *spirit*.

There is a reason your Sun sign is otherwise known as your Star Sign - it's because, quite simply, the Sun *is* a star; in fact, it's the largest, brightest, shiniest one in Earth's known visible Universe. This book is about your Sun sign and how you can become much larger, glow with far more brilliance, and shine brighter than you ever dreamed possible. I wish you all the magic in the galaxy for your dreams to come true and your deepest wishes to become reality, through tapping into the amazing power and inherent potential of your Sun sign. So get set for a galactical ride through the lucky stars of your constellation - and may a shooting star cross the path in front of you as you go!

LIBRA THE SCALES

★ Cardinal Air, Masculine, Positive, Thinking ★

"Equilibrium is achieved through relationship"

Body & Health
Kidneys, Skin, Glands, Adrenals, Lumbar Area of Spine, Acid/Alkaline, Sugar & Temperature Balance, Lower Back.

How Libra Emanates its Life Force / Energy
Elegantly, fairly, sociably, with charm

Is Concerned With
★ Partnerships, Relationships, Other People ★
★ Ideas, Opinions ★ Diplomacy ★ Politics ★
★ Balance, Romance, Harmony ★ Aesthetics ★
★ Tact ★ Self-control ★ Debate, Argument ★
★ Good Manners ★ Personal Appearance ★
★ Refinement ★ Good Taste ★ Sophistication ★
★ Rational Thought ★ Sociability ★

Spiritual Libra

Your Archetypal Universal Qualities
The Harmoniser, Diplomat, Relator

What You Refuse
To be alone or unfair

What You Are an Authority On
Relationships, art, diplomacy and etiquette

The Main Senses Through Which You Experience Your Reality
Balance, harmony, justice, beauty, cooperation

How You Love
Romantically, with grace

Positive Characteristics
★ Uses intellect ★ Cooperative ★
★ Sense of fair play ★ Artistic ★
★ Elegant ★ Good companion ★ Refined ★
★ Excellent negotiator and mediator ★
★ Charming and sociable ★ Good taste ★
★ Communicative ★ Loving ★ Romantic ★
★ Developed sense of aesthetic awareness ★

Negative Characteristics
★ Narcissistic ★ Indolent and sulky ★
★ Overbearing, overtalkative ★ Fearful ★
★ Indecisive ★ Too agreeable ★ Avoiding ★
★ Manipulative ★ Tries too hard to please ★
★ Flirtatious ★ Untrustworthy ★ Insincere ★
★ Lazy ★ Co-dependent ★ Evasive ★
★ Emotionally elusive ★

To Bring Out Your Best

Host stylish dinner parties; act as a mediator between warring parties; nurture your relationships; live in beautiful surroundings; learn how to balance work with lifestyle.

Spiritual Goals

To learn the meaning of sincere charm minus the nervous trying-too-hard-to-impress chatter; to be more reflective and less dependent on others for your personal happiness; to be more personal in your interactions and therefore come across as more genuine; to cultivate a greater sense of self and ego strength; and to learn the value and virtues of solitude and independence.

LIBRA

22 September - 22 October

Cardinal Air

Ruled by Venus

"I BALANCE"

Gemstones ◊ Opal, Tourmaline, Sapphire

★ Diplomatic, indecisive, elegant, romantic, articulate, cultured, impressionable, sociable, charming, easy going, artful, refined, flirtatious, considerate, pleasant, gullible, lazy, manipulative, impartial, procrastinating, fair, trusting, graceful, gentile, aesthetic, popular, tactful, changeable, relating, peaceable, likeable, idealistic, compromising, extravagant, hedonistic, tasteful, self-indulgent ★

"The future belongs to those who believe
in the beauty of their dreams"
Eleanor Roosevelt

LIBRA

♎

★ Elegant ★ Refined ★ Graceful ★
★ Sociable ★ Agreeable ★ Indecisive ★
★ Romantic ★ Charming

Libra is the sign of the Scales, an instrument that keeps its harmony and equilibrium only when in balance. Elegant, beautiful, refined, artful, well-versed, aesthetic, pleasant, polite, sociable, graceful and indecisive are Libras' most notable traits. Being a mentally-oriented Air sign, Librans are in love with love, and enjoy being engaged in conversation and social interaction. They are at their best when around other people; partnerships, whether they be in the form of marriage, business or a close friendship, are where they excel. Fair and tactful, Librans are masters at diplomacy and impartiality, making them great mediators and peacemakers. The Scales are also known to be fence-sitters when it comes to debate, conflict, argument and crossroads in life, finding it difficult to find or assert their opinions. Relationships are a big thing for the romantic Scales' spirit, and he constantly needs love, marriage and an 'other' to make him feel complete. Libra is charming, eloquent and tasteful, with a great appreciation for art, beauty and the finer things life has to offer. A considerate and well-versed lover, easy going friend and an idealistic charmer, Libra is the seventh sign and the most pleasant and well-liked guest at any social event, who enchants all in his presence with his gentle, agreeable and good-humoured nature.

KEY CONCEPTS
★ Incapable of decision ★
★ Hedonistic and pleasure-seeking ★
★ Relationship-seeking for personal gain ★
★ Impartial and balanced mind ★
★ Cleverly and subtly manipulative and dominating ★
★ Superficial and deceitful for own ends ★
★ Charming ★
★ Inspiring of the talents of others ★
★ Refined, artistic nature ★
★ Elegantly poised and graceful ★
★ Gregarious, affable and sociable ★
★ Ethereally intellectual ★
★ Oriented towards marriage and partnership ★

SOME CORRESPONDENCES THAT ARE ASSOCIATED WITH LIBRA

Cosmetics, florists, beauty, partnerships, dressmakers, harmony, peace, affection, grace, jewellery, aesthetics, decorators, balance, debate, arbitration, diplomats, scales, music, beauty parlours, marriage, elegance, ornaments, art, flowers, intermediaries, artists, luxury, furnishings, jewellers, love, the kidneys, weighing up, comfort, fancy goods, negotiations, pleasure, milliners, contracts, dinner parties, symmetry, beauticians, compromise, boutiques, diplomacy, embroidery, fashion, justice, social occasions, equilibrium, strategy and tact. Take your pick and enjoy the ride!

QUOTES BY LIBRANS

"Love, having no geography, knows no boundaries" - Truman Capote (30 September 1924)

"I refuse to join any club that would have me as a member" - Groucho Marx (2 October 1890)

"Live as if you were to die tomorrow. Learn as if you were to live forever" - Mahatma Gandhi (2 October 1869)

"Everyone has a responsibility towards the larger family of man, but especially if you're privileged, that increases your responsibility" - Susan Sarandon (4 October 1946)

"Women are made to be loved, not understood" - Oscar Wilde (16 October 1854)

"The secret to my success is that I bit off more than I could chew and chewed as fast as I could" - Paul Hogan (8 October 1939)

"A conversation is a dialogue, not a monologue. That's why there are so few good conversations; due to scarcity, two intelligent talkers seldom meet" - Truman Capote

"If you want something said, ask a man. If you want something done, ask a woman" - Margaret Thatcher (13 October 1925)

"When I was young, I thought that money was the most important thing in life; now that I'm old, I know that it is" - Oscar Wilde

"Where there is love, there is life" - Mahatma Gandhi

"I think it's a mistake to ever look for hope outside of oneself" - Arthur Miller (17 October 1915)

"No man goes before his time - unless the boss leaves early" - Groucho Marx

"There are two things to aim at in life: first, to get what you want; and after that, to enjoy it. Only the wisest achieve the second" - Logan Pearshall Smith (18 October 1865)

"Standing in the middle of the road is very dangerous; you get knocked down by the traffic from both sides" - Margaret Thatcher

"Trust is hard to come by. That is why my circle is close and tight" - Eminem (17 October 1972)

"A dreamer is one who can only find his way by moonlight, and his punishment is that he sees the dawn before the rest of the world" - Oscar Wilde

"Whatever your dream is, every extra penny you have needs to be going to that" - Will Smith (25 September 1968)

"No one should negotiate their dreams. Dreams must be free to fly high … You should never agree to surrender your dreams" - Jesse Jackson (8 October 1941)

"To me, the greatest pleasure of writing is not what it's about, but the inner music that words make" - Truman Capote

"Marriage is a wonderful institution, but who wants to live in an institution?" - Groucho Marx

"People think that at the top there isn't much room. They tend to think of it as Everest. My message is that there is tons of room at the top" - Margaret Thatcher

"Life is what happens while you're busy making other plans" - John Lennon (9 October 1940)

"Dealing with backstabbers, there was one thing I learned. They're only powerful when you've got your back turned" - Eminem

"Life is really simple, but we insist on making it complicated" - Confucius

"Intuition is a spiritual faculty, and does not explain, but simply points the way" - Florence Scovel Shinn (24 September 1871)

"Education is an admirable thing, but it is well to remember from time to time that nothing that is worth knowing can be taught" - Oscar Wilde

"Silence is a true friend who never betrays" - Confucius

"I have had a perfectly wonderful evening, but this wasn't it" - Groucho Marx

"The greatness of a nation and its moral progress can be judged by the way its animals are treated" - Mahatma Gandhi

"Only those who risk going too far can find out how far one can go" - T.S. Eliot (26 September 1888)

"I am so clever that sometimes I don't understand a single word of what I am saying" - Oscar Wilde

"Reality leaves a lot to the imagination" - John Lennon

"Start a huge, foolish project, like Noah. It makes absolutely no difference what people think of you" - Rumi (30 September 1207)

"We are all in the gutter, but some of us are looking at the stars" - Oscar Wilde

"Choose a job you love, and you will never have to work a day in your life" - Confucius

"Be the change you wish to see in the world" - Mahatma Gandhi

"Where there is pain, cures will be found. Where there is poverty, wealth will be supplied. Where there are questions, answers will be given. Spend less time worrying, and more time trusting" - Rumi

"Go placidly amid the chaos and haste, and remember what peace there may be in silence … Be yourself … With all its sham, drudgery and broken dreams, it is still a beautiful world. Be careful. Strive to be happy" - *Desiderata*, (Latin: 'desired things'), Max Ehrmann (26 September 1872)

"Run from what's comfortable. Forget safety. Live where you fear to live. Destroy your reputation. Be notorious" - Rumi

"Wherever you go, go with all your heart" - Confucius

"Imagine all the people, living life in peace. You may say I'm a dreamer, but I'm not the only one. I hope someday you'll join us, and the world will be as one" - John Lennon

"My life is my message" - Mahatma Gandhi

THE LIBRA CONSTELLATION

The signs of the zodiac are the twelve symbolic features that ancient people imagined while observing the heavens. They saw shapes, patterns, faces, and natural and supernatural beings in the stars, from which they established, over centuries, a kind of celestial hierarchy and system based upon their observations. Groupings of stars became constellations, and twelve of these constellations make up the zodiac, a Greek word meaning 'circle of animals', that we know today.

Star constellations are not really self-contained groups but are particularly bright stars that give the appearance of being close together and form distinctive patterns. These are the patterns that over the ages have been identified as animals, deities or mythological figures and heroes. The stars are the living past. We receive their light long after it has left the star itself and so they are a good focus for escaping from the parameters of time. Their stellar influence is analogous with the aura, the bio/psychic energy field surrounding humans, animals, plants, crystals and even places. These individual energy systems interact with the energy waves emanated by other people, and even the cosmic rays emitted by planetary bodies, for psychic energies are not limited by time or distance.

The cluster of stars we know as Libra the Scales, the only constellation not named after a living thing, has no truly bright stars, and in ancient times was not distinguished as a separate constellation, its two brightest stars belonging to the neighbouring constellation of Scorpius, as the claws of the Scorpion *. Libra is the smallest of the constellations, and is an unremarkable grouping, but is easily found by its relative position to its more noteworthy neighbours: luminous Scorpio and extensive, ethereal Virgo.

* Libra contains the northern and southern claws, two bright stars that were once part of Scorpius.

WISHING UPON YOUR STAR

The practice of wishing upon a star is familiar to most of us, and is a mystical superstition that is ingrained in many of us from childhood. As a night-time ritual, you can wish upon your own sign's constellation or that of the sign whose energies you wish to call forth; indeed, you can wish upon any constellation you feel an affinity with. If you can't see a particular constellation in your night sky, you can always meditate on it in your mind, or you can use the traditional technique of wishing upon the first star you see, while reciting the popular rhyme: *Star light, star bright, first star I see tonight, I wish I may, I wish I might, have the wish I make this night!* Any one of the three rituals will hold power for your own special wish. Good luck!

THE LIBRAN SYMBOL ♎

Astrology uses symbols or 'glyphs' to represent the planets and signs. The glyph is made up of shapes representing the energy and physical matter of which the Universe is composed, and how these shapes are used in each symbol provide hints as to the properties of the sign or planet it represents.

The ancient view was that there were five elements: Fire, Water, Air, Earth and Ether (or Spirit). Ether is invisible energy, while the four tangible elements are known as 'matter'. Ether, as pure energy, cannot be influenced by any of the physical/matter elements, although it surrounds them and indeed fuels them. The Greek philosopher and scientist Aristotle regarded this idea as a circle (Ether/Spirit) with a cross (matter) in the centre. This glyph is used in astrology as a symbol for Earth, and the cycle of life. All the symbols used in astrology represent the relationship between energy and the 'matter' elements.

The glyph of Libra represents the setting Sun, showing that the essence of being is projected into the world of the 'not-self'. It also recalls the beam of a pair of scales - Libra is Latin for a pound, suggesting that the self is to be weighed against the not-self and some kind of balance and equilibrium is to be struck between the objective and subjective consciousness. The Sun is about to sink below the horizon, symbolising the in-drawing of the life forces after the activity of spring and high summer. Evocative of the declining Sun on the horizon, this links in with Libra's coinciding with the autumn Equinox and the start of shorter days. The symbol of the Scales further emphasises that the main function of this sign is to establish equilibrium and to maintain a balance between the conflicting forces of good and evil.

The glyph for Libra also hints at its dualism. There are three recognised dual signs: Gemini, Sagittarius and Pisces. But Libra is also endowed with a certain dualism and indeed its symbol illustrates its two polarising extremes, as described previously. The upper line of the symbol shows the higher nature of Libra, which is primarily influenced by higher powers of intellect: the objective state of mind, which is the impartial aspect of the Libran character which is not attached to form or matter but is solely interested in the flow of ideas. But the lower part of the glyph represents matter, and so it reveals this struggle with the dualism inherent in our human nature; the essence of Libra therefore, is to teach others as well as himself, and how to balance the two opposing urges or forces within himself, with the condition of his Earthly affairs.

It has also been said that Libra's glyph could depict a bird, its outstretched wings parallel with the horizontal plane of the Earth but never quite touching it.

The symbol of Libra, represented by these two parallel and horizontal lines, the top one being slightly curved upwards in its centre, is usually interpreted to be the two pans and central arm of a pair of scales. The lower line symbolises the physical, while the upper the metaphysical. The two lines never touch, but Libra is not only intellectual but also soulful - as shown by the Lunar crescent atop.

THE AGE OF LIBRA ★ 14,000 - 12,000 BC

The Age of Libra brought a sense of balance and harmony to the world. Very little is known about this time, which lies deep in prehistory. It was around the time of the end of the last major Ice Age, when the climate of the Earth was beginning to become more moderate and less extreme - an apt reflection of the Libran trait of moderation and balance. Qualities of equilibrium and harmony - which correspond with Libra - were certainly needed and much-welcomed during this period. Humanity had been facing extreme, harsh living conditions up until this point, but these aspects of the world were finally starting to dissipate and humans were able to begin to establish more settled, orderly societies, which is evidenced by the fact there were larger and more numerous settlements formed at this time than at any other previous age. Cave painting was at a peak during the Age of Libra, and there was also a development of creating portable art, such as jewellery. Decorative spears, carvings of game animals, and ancient musical instruments such as flutes which have been discovered from this period, serve to further reflect Libra's ruling of the arts and music.

THE RUNDOWN & LESSONS
SOME QUIRKS, ODDITIES, UNIQUE CHARACTERISTICS AND IDIOSYNCRASIES OF LIBRA

There are two types of thinkers: what I like to call 'right-brainers' and 'left-brainers'. The left hemisphere of the human brain deals with things such as control of speech, verbal functions, logic, reason, mathematics, linear concepts, details, sequences, the intellect and analysis; the right hemisphere is concerned with spatial, music, holistic, artistic concepts, as well as simultaneity and intuition. You could go on to say that the left brain is masculine or yang in quality, and the right brain is feminine or yin in quality. Based upon these very simplistic outlines, it can be further stated that Air sign Libra dwells mainly in the left hemisphere, with a healthy dose of right thrown in for good measure.

The cerebral nature of Air highlights thought rather than emotion and feeling. Libra is largely motivated by reasoning processes, combined with a sociable and intellectual grace. Positive, hot, moist, sanguine and rational, an enterprising (Cardinal) intellectual (Air) approach characterises the sign of Libra.

Libra is the second of the Airy signs, is positive in magnetism, and is ruled by the beautiful 'evening star' planet, Venus. People born under this sign are generally fair, easy going, harmonious, diplomatic and graceful. Libra seeks balanced exchange in one-on-one partnerships, using diplomacy and tact to make social efforts more effective. You are motivated by a need to see justice done, and will negotiate inexhaustibly for fairness and inclusiveness of every group and person in a community. Your smile melts even the hardest of hearts, and your charm wins over the highest of authorities, especially when it comes to presenting an argument you wholeheartedly stand for.

Libra was the last sign added to the zodiac and used to be the 'claws' of the Scorpio constellation. It constitutes something of an enigma, inasmuch as it appears to have been 'inserted' into the zodiac at a relatively late date. In Ancient Babylonia, there were only eleven signs: The Libra constellation we know today, was known as the claws of the Scorpion rather than a separate sign. The Greeks saw this star group as the scales held by a goddess of justice, which links it with Virgo rather than Libra.

The symbolic scales of Libra had a deep significance for the Egyptians. According to mythology, at the time of one's death the goddess Maat placed the human soul on one scale and a feather on the other. If the scale tipped even slightly, the soul must reincarnate with the goal of releasing the extra weight. And since Libra comes just before Scorpio, the sign associated with death and rebirth, the prime aim in life was to make the scales balance, or to prepare the soul for its afterlife.

In modern life, but still symbolically, Libra's scales are constantly weighing and measuring the quality, fairness, or justice of their social interactions and all-important relationships (Libra's scales are always slightly tipped away from the self and towards others). Libra marks the beginning of the second half of the zodiac, and as such launches us into the less personal and more interpersonal realms of the human experience.

Libra is the only sign represented by an inanimate object. It naturally occupies the Seventh House of partnerships and is the first sign above the horizon, which can also symbolically represent its ruling of the kidneys. While Aries, its direct opposite, is associated with 'birth', Libra symbolises the birth of our-self through others. Being an Air sign, Libra has a need for personal space but he also needs social interaction and exchange. Libra places a great emphasis on relationships, and uses his mind, charm and innate sociability to connect with others. Libra instinctively knows that creating and sharing experiences with others has much more bearing on him than the solitary state. In fact, you are neither a King (Leo) or a servant (Virgo) and your ego seems to grow by reflection; the more love you are surrounded by, the brighter your personality shines. Not a leader, nor a follower, you are democratic and prefer cooperative effort, for you always desire to be part of a collective force of movement. Unlike Gemini, whose approach is impersonal and scattered, and Aquarius, whose approach is group-focused and detached, you are able to integrate others into your experience for your own personal gain, as well as to help them further themselves. In fact, you are a perfect social organiser, and know how to blend many diverse characters into a functioning, coordinated whole.

Your Cardinal quality means that mental rapport and intellectual compatibility are a strong feature in your associations with others. In fact, Libra cannot bear to be at odds with anyone. You have a driving desire to secure peace and harmony at all costs, for you cannot bear discord, the ugliness of confrontation or the responsibility of causing pain, and you are perfectly prepared to compromise your ideals in pursuit of this. With a natural charm and pleasant nature bestowed upon you by your ruling planet Venus, you rarely fail to achieve this goal. But Libra is not primarily concerned with intimate or romantic relationships, for there is always a sense of higher purpose lingering in the background. Libra, an Air sign, plants the seeds for a broader vision of humanity, a vision which comes full circle in the next Air sign Aquarius.

Despite your Airy temperament which lends itself to a certain kind of detachment, there's a certain deep richness to a Libran's emotions, no matter what kind of feeling is high, low or ascending at any given moment, and a philosophic approach to both joys and sadness that rarely fails to smooth things out in the end. Indeed, your instinct for sanity and righting wrongs sees to that, and as a result it is a rare Libran who suffers breakdowns of any kind. Having said that, harmony of the mind, body and spirit doesn't always come easily to you.

Libra is not a dualistic sign, but there are some contradictions and paradoxes inherent in your character nonetheless. You can be fair and argumentative at the same time; as well as rich and humble; good-natured but sulky; impartial yet quarrelsome; pleasant but indolent; active then lazy; intelligent but naïve; trusting yet snobbish; restless but unhurried; and smart yet gullible. Librans can be very confusing and possess a frustrating inconsistency that baffles others, particularly those striving towards the 'textbook balanced Scales' character they've read and heard so much about!

Libra is the only non-animal sign of the zodiac, signifying that it is the most removed from the primal, instinctive side of life. Librans have a need to be objective and try hard to be impartial and believe in the importance of a level playing field. The Libran scales are constantly used to weigh up whether or not a situation or person is being fair, and to decide if justice is being served. If not, Librans see it as their noble duty to rectify any imbalance, and that is why, far from being compliant and indecisive, they can sometimes be outspoken and strident. Determined to put right injustices and restore balance and harmony, you will be opinionated and even argumentative when the mood, moment or circumstances call for it.

Contrary to popular opinion, and despite the fact that Libra's glyph is the Scales, Libra is rarely well balanced. In fact, you're quite the opposite - your mood and opinion will swing first one way, then the opposite until, in time, an evenness is achieved. This process of striving for balance can be long and arduous for the long-suffering Scales, who has to actively explore all the options and consider all the possibilities before making a decision. Although you are often cited as being the most levelled sign of the zodiac, you are tougher than you appear and sometimes you are just adapting, adjusting or compromising in order to make others happy, rather than as a result of supposed inner harmony. Although you are a vacillating sign who can swing wildly between extremes or sit on the fence, ultimately your god is logic and you subject everything in your life to your reasoning processes; discounting feelings and mistrusting intuition, you usually rely only on rationale. No other considerations seem to apply for you, which can sometimes be to your detriment. You have an agile mind that is capable of abstract thought and discerning judgement, and you show great flair for planning, strategy and debating. However, you are not a coldly calculating detached robot either. Ruled by Venus, whose gentle and softening influence endows you with the abilities to relate and reconcile, your glyph can also be seen as a bridge - a symbol of linkage, or a rising Sun, representing options and possibilities. Your main weakness is that you usually strive to see *all* sides of any picture, and any pressure to make a decision is experienced as stress. You always want to get it just right, to be fair.

You can achieve much with your words, as you are the tactful diplomat of the zodiac. You know the value of compromise and accomplish more through gentle persuasion than the more overt tactics of your fellow Cardinal signs Aries, Cancer and Capricorn. Being of the intellectual Air trilogy, you are skilled at thinking about, weighing up and assessing the pros and cons of any situation in order to reach a fair result or judicious verdict.

Your romantic life can fluctuate between the soaring heights of blissful union and the deepest trenches of loneliness. As you are largely motivated by your ruler Venus, you dream of a perfect partner, creating a complete relationship, and are constantly seeking that soul connection - but what you are *exactly* looking for is never quite clear as it changes so much in yourself. Also, because you are seeking the elusive perfect lover and nothing less than a god or goddess, you are often disappointed in the mere mortals who show up in your life in response to your requests. And once you land yourself in an unwanted relationship, you can encounter extreme difficulties in untangling yourself, as you are so adverse to break-ups of any kind. In these cases, you may even use your powers of subtle persuasion and manipulation to create situations in order to make the other person break the bond, rather than you having to do it yourself - severance is *not* your forte. Although the element of Air lends you a certain detachment, when it comes to relationships, your deep desire for love can lead to intense emotions, even outbursts, sulking and tantrums. But generally, you would prefer to avoid messy feelings and anything which may cause conflicts or jeopardise your chances of a harmonious partnership. You may even fail to see the other for who they really are - faults, weaknesses, warts and all. You tend to put your lovers on a pedestal and refuse to recognise their true colours, pure natures or the deeper core of their being. This has largely to do with your own personal projections onto the relationship, but also has to do with your idealism.

In pursuit of relationship perfection, you will overlook flaws and gloss over problems; this seeking can be so acute that you over-compromise, which leads to deep dissatisfaction. Plus, there is a little-known touch of pride in the Libran nature, which doesn't like others to see the more vulnerable side of his inner self, which definitely exists but is always hidden under his cool, graceful-under-pressure exterior. You can also be lazy and inefficient, which can hinder your passion, zest and progress in relationships, although these traits are normally overlooked in favour of your many desirable qualities.

Sociable Venus seeks to harmonise and unify and this is translated into romantic magnetism. Whereas your fellow Air sign Gemini is concerned with making connections, Libra has a very strong need to form relationships, to give and to receive loving affection, and to relate to another. Through a partner, you are in some way able to 'validate' yourself and therefore better able to express your sense of self. Further, you cannot bear to be on bad terms with anyone. Your need for popularity, approval and the constant approbation of others is paramount, and there is nothing you would not do in order to safeguard these.

For the most part though, Libra represents the part of the zodiacal mandala where we are concerned with the primary mating relationship and the balancing of this partnership with the needs of the self, which perpetually poses difficult challenges to the human psyche. Libra is known for his inability to make a decision because he can see both sides of any situation and always strives to be fair and balanced. The most challenging task for the Libran is to see things from a self-centred position, and therefore he is often too self-sacrificing when concerned with his significant other. Libra, after all, is the Sun's 'fall' position, where the ego diffuses and dilutes itself in favour of the other. And most Librans will find their centre and rejuvenation best in the company of their favourite partner or people - talking, laughing, sharing and discussing.

Despite your constant trying to keep your Scales at the same level, there is one aspect of your life in which you don't always experience much-sought-after balance: that of eating, drinking and enjoying yourself. Many Librans indulge in excessive eating, drinking or enjoying themselves a little *too* much, which manifest themselves in such undesirable states as promiscuous behaviour, weight gain and alcohol-induced regrets. When you upset your balance and find yourself out of kilter, you can compensate by repeating the cycles until something forces you to examine your-self in a deeper way, which isn't one of your fortes. Librans are quite happy skipping along the surface of life, thank you very much!

You can also take your justice-seeking and fairness to extremes at times, and they can become almost obsessional traits. Your ability to see all sides can be a weakness or a strength, depending on how you use it. You dislike making instant decisions without taking all the possibilities into consideration, and this can be seen as stalling, or worse, procrastination, another one of your more negative characteristics. Many a fence has been worn down by your backside sitting squarely upon it, refusing to budge until you've weighed up the pros and cons of each side. The strength in this lies in the fact that you make a fine mediator, and make considered decisions when you do finally arrive at one; certainly, no one could ever accuse Libra of being rash, flighty, impulsive or hasty when it comes to a crossroads. All directions are worthy of your attention and consideration. You don't like to be pushed, coerced or hurried while you're deciding on the course either.

Fence-sitting can lead to blandness of character. But this can work for *and* against you; Libra concentrates on what is expected and fair, but this can lead to a lack of personal integrity and you can easily get lost in trying to do the right thing and maintaining the status quo. Libra represents the urge to merge, share, exchange ideas and forge unions, and although you have a competitive streak it is always fought in a battlefield among equals and you find it important and gratifying to share the outcome.

Very few Librans are eccentric, showy or outlandish. Rather, you are wholesome, peaceable, refined, deliberate and careful. Diplomatic, tolerant, equalitarian and appreciative of arts and beauty, Libra is concerned with symmetry, aesthetics and evenness. You prefer ideas over feelings, enjoy one-on-one sharing, have utopian thought, are judgemental but fair-minded, never condemn, have a detached sense of judgement, and you are great at people-watching and assessing. Sociable, sophisticated, refined, you can also be anxious, unable to confront, and talk in riddles if you find something difficult to say, and are competitive but do not like direct competition.

To the Libran outward appearances are important; dignity, composure and poise are paramount. You have a strong dislike of things which are sordid, ugly or distasteful. You abhor vulgarity, exaggeration and embarrassing displays of anger and passion.

Libra speaks lucidly and intellectually about feelings and is known to be insincere but in a charming way. You don't often show it, but Librans have a fantastic ability to concentrate and to ponder deep subjects. Overall, you are an artistic soul at heart. You have a strong desire to be with others and to share, create unions, and cooperate. But you can be shallow and *too* easy going, which may leave you open to manipulation. However, you have a tendency towards being manipulative *towards* others, particularly if it is to avoid confronting an unsavoury situation. You are the most adept sign at noticing beauty and pick up on aspirations of the human spirit. You are easily influenced by and intellectually idolise others, even though you are an intellectual and well-rounded thinker yourself. You are passive/aggressive and tend to get what you want without actually asking. Diplomacy is your forte and negotiating with results comes naturally to you; you find it easy to persuade other people to carry out tasks and little jobs for you, although, being initiating and Cardinal in nature, you will just as happily do the job yourself if no one is around. Your love of beauty, relationships and art is more of an ideal than a total involvement or immersement; appreciation of such pleasures is done with composure rather than passion and intensity.

Ultimately, Libra represents cooperation in its highest expression, however competitive. A word of caution though, once the battle is over and neither side has won nor lost but both emerge triumphant, do not disturb the Libran's need to restore his own inner peace, for nothing upsets the delicate see-saw of your Scales more.

Inside anyone who has a strong Libran influence in their natal chart, is someone who is terrified of being alone. Romantic and charming, you are the most relationship-focused of all the Air signs, and your desire for balance and cooperation can enliven any partnership. Librans function at their best when relating to and working alongside others, for they need someone with whom to share and communicate with; without this they can easily become lost wandering souls, and tend towards promiscuity or misguided decisions that may erode their self-esteem. Thankfully, however, Libran's natural charm and sociability rarely finds them truly alone. Although intelligent and quite shrewd in business matters, they are also secretly gullible and more easily influenced than they would want others to believe.

At times you may aim for artificial harmony, and this, combined with your indecision and impeccable manners can in fact alienate others instead of winning them over; your insincerity is often detectable. You are most true to your style and sense of fair play when you choose to accept the disharmonies, speak your truth and still uplift the tone of social situations regardless.

LESSONS TO BE LEARNED FOR GREATER POWER, ENLIGHTENMENT & LUCK

Libran problems and ultimate undoings arise through over-compromise, over-agreeableness, indecisiveness, laziness, idealistic rose-coloured-glasses, dependence on the company of others, and the need to be in a relationship. Well known as the peaceful, harmonious sign, Libra can sometimes be surprisingly selfish, incorporating the more obnoxious traits of its opposite, Aries. You can be self-serving, overindulgent, hedonistic and shallow, with an overemphasis on beauty, image and the need to fit in. Libra's shadow side can make them lie, manipulate and cheat in an effort to keep up appearances. Because you are so focused on relationships, you have a tendency to adapt *too* much, often to the detriment of yourself and your happiness. Libra needs ultimately to learn a little more separation from others in order to develop into a more decisive and assertive individual.

Libra's greatest strength is found in the forming of soul-satisfying, creative relationships with individuals and with your environment. If your relationships are not serving you or turn sour, your weaknesses can emerge. So tuned in to partnership you are, that if alone you may feel lost unless you begin to make your life your work of art. You can find the beauty and balance you so crave when your love includes the wider world. When you withdraw and brood on what you haven't got, you tend to reach out to others with a false pride and insincerity based upon insecurities and fear. You may also become co-dependent and risk losing your identity - and your natural dignity - in your relationships. At your best, however, you are balanced, popular, respected and self-respecting, able to create inspiring connections that combine independence and cooperative union - and your inner peace and your outer calm will both reflect this pleasant harmony.

THE THREE DECANS OF LIBRA

Decans are thirty-six groups of stars that rise in a particular order on the horizon throughout each Earth rotation. These decans were developed in Egypt thousands of years ago. The rising of each decan marked the beginning of a new 'decanal hour' of the night for these ancient people, and eventually three decans were assigned to each zodiac sign. Each decan covers ten degrees of the zodiac wheel, and is ruled by different planetary rulers that rule over the other two signs of the same element (and a traditional ruler, when only seven of the planetary bodies were known). Decans continued to be used throughout the Ages, in astrology and in magic, but many modern astrologers, for whatever reasons, tend to disregard them. Following are brief descriptions for each decan of Libra. Which one do you belong to? Can you relate to the description and the energies of your decan's ruling planet?

FIRST DECAN LIBRA ★ September 22 - October 2

Ruler ★ Moon (traditional *) / Venus (modern)

Keyword ★ Sociable

First Decan Libra's Three Special Tarot Cards
Justice, Queen of Swords & Two of Swords

Birthdays in this decan range from 23rd September to 2nd October. This is the Libra decan, ruled by the Moon * and Venus, which means that love, more or less, fills the lives and thoughts of those born under its influence. Charming and attractive, you can easily attract others to you and make a good impression on others, and are indeed at your best when you are surrounded by a wide variety of people. Peace loving, romantic, clever and imaginative, you have good communication skills and the innate capacity to rise to great heights in the creative fields. You love to create harmony in relationships and, with a heightened sense of aesthetic awareness, enjoy being surrounded by beautiful things. Deeply intuitive and attuned to your own and others' feelings, you seek harmony and attachment, and peace is very important to you; conflict is usually avoided altogether. Overall, you are affable, kind affectionate and artistic.

SECOND DECAN LIBRA ★ October 3 - 13

Ruler ★ Saturn (traditional *) / Saturn (modern)

Keyword ★ Easy going

Second Decan Libra's Three Special Tarot Cards
Justice, Queen of Swords & Three of Swords

Birthdays in this decan range from 3rd October to 13th October. This is the Aquarius decan, ruled by Saturn *. Librans born during this decan are strongly sensual and attractive, with a more heightened intelligence and power to influence than Librans born under other decans. Thoughtful, contemplative and serious, you have the ability to take on the world. The Saturnian influence endows you with a determination, perseverance and decisiveness, and you are usually successful in achieving your ambitions or aspirations, using your natural wit, charm and shrewdness. You are patient and responsible, but sometimes take too much upon yourself and become weighed down with worry and burdens, which, under your calm and cool exterior, you rarely share with others.

THIRD DECAN LIBRA ★ October 14 - 22

Ruler ★ Jupiter (traditional *) / Mercury (modern)

Keyword ★ Fair

Third Decan Libra's Three Special Tarot Cards
Justice, King of Cups & Four of Swords

Birthdays in this decan range from 14th October to 22nd October. This is the Gemini decan, ruled by Jupiter * and Mercury. Librans born during this decan are characterised by idealism, charm and romanticism. You love to explore many fascinating ideas and interests, and often attract good fortune through the use of your mind and clever way with words. Bright, eloquent, articulate, breezy and charismatic, you enjoy attention from others and sharing your thoughts, affection and concepts. With Jupiter's benevolent influence, you are likely to be generous and to seek compromise, justice and fairness at all costs. The quest or ethical and aesthetic values is ever present, and you enjoy a constant whirl of stimulating conversations and social events, as your happiness and harmony depend upon these. Overall, you have a great thirst for knowledge and are able to combine logic and intuition with effortless ease, magnetising all manner of auspicious circumstances and people to you.

* The decan's traditional ruler based on the Chaldean order of the planets

YOUR ELEMENT ★ AIR

According to the *Oxford English Dictionary*, the word *element* has a mysterious origin, and was first found in Greek texts meaning 'complex whole' or 'a single unit made up of many parts'. From the ancient up to medieval times, there were only four elements - Earth, Air, Fire and Water - and the occult-oriented also believed in a fifth: Spirit, or Ether. (Cornelius Agrippa called Spirit the 'quintessence'.)

Alchemy is a tradition of visions and dreams, and images can combine on different levels of reality. Alchemists have long used images in their illustrations to express the enigma and mystery of their art, and to include all dimensions of our experience. The traditional worlds of Earth, Water, Fire and Air symbolise these dimensions very well. Broadly speaking, and in human terms, Earth corresponds to the level of the body and the senses, Water to the flow of thoughts and feelings, Fire to inspiration and energy, and Air to the world of the higher mind. Each of these worlds has its own realm of imagery. Libra belongs to the realm of the Air element.

★ The Intellectual Group ★

The path to BROTHERHOOD

Focused on Mental & Social Interactions

Alchemical Associations ★ The Intellect, Gold and the Colour Yellow

Key Attributes ★ Communication, Intelligence, Reason, Perspective, Renewal, Thought, Logic

Symbolism ★ Clear Thought, Communication, Study, Connection to the Universals

Governed by ★ The Mind and the Psyche

Air Characteristics ★ Intelligent, Wise, Thoughtful, Analytical, Detached, Objective

★ THE MAGIC OF AIR ★

Many Eastern philosophies believe that the vital force that energises both humans and the cosmos is carried in the Air, entering our bodies when we breathe. This fundamental energy is called *prana* in India, *chi* in China and *ki* in Japan. Spiritual prayers from Buddhist prayer flags are believed to be carried in the wind.

Air is invisible and intangible, but it drives life and is necessary to animate all living things. Represented by sky, wind, flight and breath, Air can be a cool breeze, fanning the flames of desire, or a strong wind, creating a hurricane. Taking deep breaths can calm and soothe the spirits. Air represents your intellect - the ambitions that are driven by a cool detachment from your emotions. Air seeks out what you need more than what you want and fans you gently along, rather than sweeps you off your feet with the dreams, force or illusions of Water or Fire; Air rationalises your desires. It also refreshes and purifies you, blowing away your problems and carrying you towards new solutions - by being literally a 'breath of fresh air' in your experiences.

★ KEYWORDS ★

Broad-minded, fair, objective, refined, ideas-oriented, communicative, observant, versatile, rational, theoretical, social, learning-oriented, impersonal, logical, innovative, connective, detached, active-minded, clever, curious, impartial, cooperative, abstract, integrating, networking, analytical, relationship-oriented, intellectual

Air is the mental principle. The most intellectual and innovative of the four elements, it is unconcerned with the material side of life, but rather it seeks to share with and communicate ideas to others. It is a connective energy, driven to share thought and mental rapport. Air is associated with the thinking function and its motivating force is mind-thought stimulation. Characterised by intellect and aspiration over passion, Airy types are ideas people, using rational and logical thought processes, seeking mental understanding and experiencing life through the mind. They are also objective and 'head-orientated', sometimes to the detriment of their emotions and intuition.

The three Air signs are Gemini the Twins, Libra the Scales and Aquarius the Water Bearer. In the horoscope wheel, Gemini represents personal development, Libra represents interpersonal development, and Aquarius represents transpersonal development. The Air signs, living in world of communication and the intellect, express themselves in these differing ways: Gemini, through its quickness to see both sides of any issue and to create original thoughts from what has been learned; Libra, through its ability to balance many different viewpoints and find a harmonious consensus and keep the status quo; and Aquarius, through its foresight and vision to understand the Universal principles that can be used for the betterment of mankind. The Air signs are masculine in polarity, extroverted in expression, and are aligned with the realms of relationships and connections of all kinds.

Air is perhaps the most misunderstood of the elements, because of its intangible nature and lack of visible manifestation. However, without Air there can be no Fire; Water devoid of oxygen is merely hydrogen gas; and in the absence of Air there is simply no conscious, breathing life. Air represents the insubstantial state of mind of cognisance. As a progressive chain of development, elemental Air is the final stage of spiritual evolution. Fire is the first creative spark, which coalesces into the nurturing Waters of life and growth, Earth the solid, corporeal plane of existence, but as all life is cyclical and these material states eventually wane and waste away, elemental Air remains as the soul-like auric energy or discarnate spirit. Additionally, Air is usually invisible and one only notices its effects when it is directed through another element. Indeed, Air's magical powers can be activated through Fire (smoke), Earth (moving through mobiles and wind chimes for example), and Water (inhalation, steam and vaporisation).

Air gives us life, thanks to that which we breathe in. It is both life- and death-inducing, very real and yet ambiguous. In astrology, the exact moment the newborn inhales its first breath is when we choose to establish the birth chart. But this rhythm of life is also a rhythm of death. In fact, the breath which enables a child to live independently and freed from its cord, depends on a continuous movement. At the other end of life, withholding your breath signifies drawing your last and expiring, or dying. Ultimately, breathing is a spontaneous, instinctive, vital action which allows us to exist.

The soul and breath have always been closely linked. But breath is not the soul; it is its vehicle. Both are unseen and impalpable. Breath is also the vehicle for thought, sound, spirit, speech and language. Air is the same for everyone, yet our breath is unique to us alone. Perhaps that is why those born of the Air element often have a delicate albeit superficial sensitivity to the Air around them, its nuances and temperature, its feel and its nature, its fragrance and its moisture.

Air is also associated with inspiration, ideas and exchange, representing the Divine energies and messages from the gods. Inspired by birds, shamans use spirit flight in their healing ceremonies and rituals. Air can open your mind to new possibilities and allow your imagination to take flight. All cultures have legends of wise 'messengers' descending from the air, such as angels, birds, winged dragons and science fiction aliens, all of whom, it is supposed, have access to higher sources of information than Earth-dwellers. Witches are often depicted flying through the Air on their broomsticks, a symbol of their wisdom and magic. And the sky gods of ancient times were all guardians of arcane studies and were thought to pass on these gifts to the humans who believed in as well as called upon them.

When we work with Air, we think of the Divine breath of spirit, the ability to move through space and time, and the wisdom derived from experience and study. Like the other elements, Air has three manifestations - mental, astral and physical - when used in magic and ritual. We can visualise (mental), request the use of the energy (astral), or physically create the elemental associations in our experience. Where Earth elemental magic lends itself to manifesting things in a physical form, finding treasure, creating abundance and harnessing the strength within, Air is more of a studious, mental variety: writing and telling stories, sending messages, taking (mental) notes, composing music, studying anything, and clarity of thought. Hermes, the Greek messenger god, and his Roman counterpart Mercury are both associated with the Air element.

The Air element is connected to understanding, intellectual concepts, innovations, insight, mental rapport, technology, synthesising information, ideas, communication, and knowledge. As air has no boundaries, it can be difficult for this element to accept boundaries established by others. It is objective, gives a sense of separation through interdependence, is sophisticated and is linked to the past, present *and* future. It seeks intellectual rapport and stimulation above all else, and has a conscious sense of *knowing*.

This element is detached, impersonal, separate, represents breath and life, is an ideas perfectionist, is judging, assessing, collating, paradoxical, space-seeking, freedom-seeking, flighty, has an approach/avoidance element, develops ways to communicate, is an observer/spectator, gossiper, is an excellent witness to the human experience, is an equality-idealist, is dual-natured in many ways, has difficulty with intimacy, is dissociative in the face of challenge, is aware and conscious, has an urge to relate and 'share', is socially inclined and witty, has perspective, keeps its distance, is changeable, fair, learned, inspiring and opinionated, and has an attitude of "knowledge is power."

Airy temperaments excel at clear, objective reasoning and have a capacity for lively, intelligent communication and the exchange of ideas. These types are gregarious, civilised, curious, cooperative, casual, fun-loving and sociable.

However, they can be overly intellectual, objective and rational, uncomfortable with feelings, and too often trust their heads before their hearts. Other weaknesses that may trip them up occasionally are that they have a tendency to be scattered, unfocused, unrealistic, detached, distant, impersonal, nervous, unstable, inconsistent, spacey, erratic, whimsical, fickle, impractical, superficial, opinionated, dogmatic, impulsive, skittish, 'mercurial', disembodied, a chatterbox, have an overactive mind and can't be tied down.

As the element suggests, Airy spirits are constantly on the move, shifting, changing and evolving. Air signs are generally unnerved by states of flux, as movement is a chance for growth and exploration to these inquisitive souls. Independent, open-minded and spontaneous, Air signs loathe restrictions and anything which curtails their freedom, especially of thought. They love to broaden their horizons through circulating amongst people, places and experiences, as understanding others and their surroundings is paramount to making sense of their existence.

Air signs rely heavily on reason, logic and objectivity. This enables the cerebral Air signs to make fair and objective assessments, but this intellectualisation of thought and feeling can also make them come across as detached and unemotional. As they have a strong need for novel and perpetual stimulation, Air signs tend to be restless and can suffer from nerve-related upsets. But blessed with outgoing and naturally expressive personalities, they are highly sociable as well as good communicators. Air signs enjoy the company of others and love engaging in hearty, interesting conversations through which they can gain knowledge and swap ideas. Impartial by nature, they often make great mediators in relationships or families and having an upbeat, generally uncomplicated nature means Air signs also have a natural talent for diffusing tense situations and lifting the spirits of others.

Positive Air Qualities ★ Focused on ideas and their expression, objective, tolerant, inspiring, articulate, socially adept, intelligent, cooperative, stimulating, charming, rational, relational, mentally clear, succinct, detached, perceptive, sharp, clever, gregarious, and capable of forethought, understanding and the grasping of abstract concepts.

Negative Air Qualities ★ Impractical, unemotional, lacking in sympathy, glib, non-committal, facile, hyperactive, nervous, dissociated from the body and the physical world, manipulative, flighty.

THE ARCHANGEL OF AIR ★ RAPHAEL

An archangel is an angel of greater than ordinary rank. They possess a stronger, more powerful essence than the guardian angels, through overseeing and guiding the other angels who are said to be with us here on Earth. The word 'angel' derives from the Greek word *angelos* meaning 'messenger'. To humans, angels are often seen as bringers as all sorts of messages. Angels in all their forms are believed to bring the message of 'spirit' into matter, carrying the blueprints of creation and the Source from the Divine into the manifest world. Angels are not and never have been human; they, like fairies and nature spirits, are part of a different evolutionary pattern – but they do appear to us in human form (usually with wings) because that is what we understand. An angel can be in many different places at once, and with the same intensity and concentration, and wish for us to be aware of them and benefit from them.

There are said to be three categories of angels in the cosmos, each with three subdivisions *. 'Angel' is the generic term and also relates specifically to those closest to the physical. Similarly, archangel may be taken to mean any of the higher orders, and indeed signifies the order just above ordinary 'angel'. Found in a number of religious traditions, the word 'archangel' itself is usually associated with the Abrahamic religions. The word archangel is of Greek origin, and means literally 'chief angel'. All archangels end with the 'el' suffix, 'el' meaning 'in God' and the first part of the name meaning what each individual Angel specialises in. The archangel who rules your sign will be the one with whom you most resonate. The astrological sign is an energy signature, a matrix of a specific stellar pattern that will subtly affect and influence you. Although there are many associations for the great archangels of the Universe, we must keep in mind there is great overlapping in their duties and guidance. For example, we may say that one is for healing and another for protection, but they can all perform the functions of the others, and each has only areas of greater focus and responsibilities. Four of the multitude of archangelic beings work intimately with the Earth. These are Raphael (Air), Michael (Fire), Gabriel (Water) and Uriel (Earth). Associated with each of these archangels are one of the four elements, specific colours, one of the four directions or quarters of the Earth, three signs of the zodiac, and a variety of other energies and powers. Understanding these associations and considering them in relation to our own paths, can help us determine with which of them we are more likely to resonate. Your sign, being of the Air element, vibrates to the essence of Raphael.

* The first sphere, the *Heavenly Counsellors*, comprises Seraphim, Cherubim and Thrones. The second sphere, the *Heavenly Governors*, comprises Dominions, Virtues and Powers. The third sphere, the *Heavenly Messengers*, comprises Principalities, Archangels and Angels. Of course, all such classifications are a human construct, a way of placing order upon the unknowable and allowing us to perceive something about which we have no words to express. However, as long as we think of angelic hierarchies as a way of working with celestials, of remembering important attributes, and we are able to imagine and experience these beings, this order of angels will prove useful to those wishing to draw upon their messages and assistance.

★ ARCHANGEL RAPHAEL'S ASSOCIATIONS ★

Element of Air
The eastern quarter of the Earth
The spring season
The colour blue (or blue and gold)
The astrological signs of Gemini, Libra and Aquarius

Raphael, meaning "Healing power of God" or "The Divine has healed," is the archangel of healing and safe travels. This being works to stimulate energies for overall life and success. Raphael awakens a sense of beauty, wonder and creativity which stimulates higher mental faculties. He is the supreme healer in the angelic realm, whose chief role is to support, heal and guide in all matters of health, working to heal people's minds, bodies and spirits so they can enjoy overall peace and wellbeing. Raphael is the Keeper of the Holy Grail.

LIBRA'S ZODIAC ARCHANGEL ★ CHAMUEL

Additionally, each sign is associated with a particular archangel. Such knowledge can help you to build up a relationship with these beings, based upon your strengths and needs. However, no link is rigid, and as you work with angels you will come to develop your own affinities. When invoking a specific archangel, a useful ritual to draw them closer is to light a candle in that angel's colour, burn some oil or incense of its scent, and hold the appropriate crystal while focusing on what you are needing guidance on.

YOUR ARCHANGEL ★ Chamuel is the relationship balancer and healer, enabling the heart to open and encouraging you to value yourself and realise what you have to offer. Chamuel brings comfort if a relationship is in distress, giving you the gift of insight that you still have much to offer and your love has not been wasted. He can also connect you with your soul mate.

SCENT/OIL ★ Ylang Ylang

CANDLE COLOUR ★ Soft pink

CRYSTAL ★ Rose quartz

THE DEVIC REALMS & AIR ★ EAST: REALM OF THE SYLPHS

"Through magick we do conjure the Elements, evoking unto us the special properties of the Life-force for our learning and our coming-into-light. And yet are there secret paths of knowledge that have fallen from the minds of men ... For the way of Magick is a path to sacred knowledge, of reverence and humility - and the world is a wondrous place. Yet how many amongst us have fathomed these depths?"
Merlin's Book of Magick and Enchantment, Nevill Drury

Deva is a Sanskrit word that means 'shining one'. Devas are the life force within nature, and there are four devic realms - Fire, Earth, Air and Water - which contain ethereal elemental spirits or sprites. Elementals are the building blocks of nature, and close to being true energy and consciousness. The four elements correspond to four different states of matter: energy/transmutation (Fire), gas (Air), liquid (Water) and solid (Earth), which are linked to the four human states of consciousness: inspiration, thought, feeling and practicality. There are four spirits, or elementals, which reside in the devic realms, associated with each element. People have been painting pictures, telling stories and writing about these devic realms for hundreds of years, albeit sometimes through disguised mediums such as fairy tales or children's fantasy stories like Tolkien's *Lord of the Rings*. The power of the natural world is easily observed and since ancient times primal forces have been ascribed to various spirit beings. Belief in nature spirits is of such ancient origin and is Universal; cultures everywhere have names or words to describe them. In the sixteenth century, a famous Swiss physician, alchemist and mystic called Paracelsus * defined these beings as 'Elementals', classifying them according to the element of nature they inhabit. There are four main levels of elemental beings: Gnomes (Earth), Undines (Water), Sylphs (Air), and Salamanders (Fire). The fifth element of Ether is the element from which came forth the other four, and Ether, or Spirit, has never been defined in any particular category, and encompasses the aspects and beings of all the other elements.

Elementals are usually benevolent guardian beings or spirits that look after nature's secrets and treasures in whatever part of the natural realm they occupy. They can only be seen or 'felt' by those possessing heightened psychic abilities, yet they can be summoned by those practising alchemy, spells and magic in order to harness the forces of nature for their own particular intentions. In our modern lives, it may seem as though this magic doesn't exist, but the truth is that most of us are simply less in touch with it than ever before. The consequence of this is that we are destroying vast areas of land, polluting waters, creating toxic landscapes, and disrespecting the laws of nature, which often whisper their messages softly. It is therefore important for us to look at the beauty that surrounds us with true appreciation and genuine regard, and to open ourselves up to the magic resides within it. The four devic realms can teach us much about nature; they act as custodians for the four elements, and learning to work with them is a way of attuning to all the energies and beings of nature. Elementals are four-dimensional, and have nothing to obstruct their movements. Therefore, they move as easily through matter as we do through air and space. They do require some contact with humans for their own evolution. Helping to direct them is an overseer, traditionally called the King of that element, and an archangel. Each of these elements is affiliated with one of the four directions and each elemental spirit embodies its own special energy. If you wish to re-connect and re-harmonise yourself by working with nature and its messages and lessons, you could begin by learning a little about your element's realm: Your element is Air, which is connected with the East direction and the realm of the Sylphs.

* Paracelsus is considered the most original medical thinker of the sixteenth century. His belief in supernatural beings, intuition and the invisible causes of illness helped him discover hydrogen and nitrogen. Paracelsus believed that "Elementals are unlike pure spirits for they are mortal, but they are not like man for they have no soul."

★ SYLPHS ★

Sylph is from the Greek *silphe*, and the word means 'butterfly'; these spirits control all winds. Sylphs are fairy-like spirits that inhabit the air, winds and atmosphere as well as high mountain tops (not all sylphs are restricted to living in the air, however). They are probably more closely in line with our concept of fairies and angels than the other elemental beings; and indeed, they work alongside the angels. Always active and extremely quick of movement and sound, Air Elementals are also known to be highly intelligent as they can gather vast amounts of information in a short period of time. They are aloof and detached and usually very subtle in their persuasiveness. People with strong sylph influence or activity often find that sexuality is not high on their list of priorities, and may not understand how it can be so with others. But the sylphs stimulate the expression of the creative sexual drive into other avenues of one's life, such as work or hobbies.

The sylphs are guardians of spring, the direction of the east and the wind. Therefore, they are chiefly concerned with communication, the mind, the intellect and the kingdom of the feathered and winged creatures. As the east is the doorway to new beginnings and the direction through which the sacred circle is always entered, air has a uniquely ethereal, otherworldly, wispy quality to it. It makes its presence felt through its four winds: the north brings cold and withering; the east brings new life and freshness; the south brings vitality and warmth; and the west brings fertility and gentle abundance. Air, and its various components, is our vital life force, enabling us to exist. It also supports that which flies - from birds to human-made technology. It allows fire to burn and for communication with others and with the ether to flow with ease, and stimulates our intellect so we can exercise good reason, judgment and rational thought to enhance our lives. Air makes its home in the heavens and yet it flows freely as a gift for all to share. It moves among us like an unseen visitor, giving us life and strength, and carrying our wishes into the breeze for them to return in the form of free-flowing bounty in our physical world. Air inhabits our hearts, bring joy and wisdom and knowing, and sylphs guard these mind treasures as they are pure spirits of truth and beauty whose ways are not sullied by Earthly restrictions. The King of Air is Lugh or Paralda, its archangel is Raphael, its magickal tool is the athame (which calls down the spirits into form), and its sacred ceremonial stones are Lapis Lazuli, Sapphire, Blue Topaz and Azurite. Perhaps Merlin sums up the sylph realm best: "For these beings are like unto jewels of light, their wings glistening as crystal butterflies in the first Dawn. We may see them in a dance of light upon a leaf or petal, perchance amidst the forest dells or in the hidden glades where few have ventured."

INVOKING THE AIR DEVAS

Sylphs are best contacted in high, open spaces where the wind blows freely. They can be found in wind, clouds, rain, storms, and snowflakes. If you are in need of clearer thought and memory, greater freedom or better communication skills, ask the air devas for their help. They can help guide you if you have an important exam or journey to undertake, if you have to give a speech, or if you are doing anything that requires clear, swift thought and self-expression. To make contact with a sylph, make or acquire a dream catcher. A Native American craft, usually hoop-shaped with dangling beads and feathers, these are designed to 'catch' bad dreams and protect you while you sleep. Dream catchers can be adapted to attract sylphs however, although they can never really be caught, since they embody the essence of liberty and unencumbered flight. Perhaps you could get a new dream catcher for this very purpose, and imbue it with your positive intentions through a special affirmation. When you become aware of your sylph stirring your dream catcher, ask for the specific help you are requiring, thank the sylph for his or her help, then set them free back into their realm of flight and freedom, knowing that their help has been given and their work done. Sylphs also respond well to the burning of incense and music.

THE EAST DIRECTION'S CORRESPONDENCES

If you wish to work more with your particular element and direction, the following may help propel your wishes and magical journey:

Time of Day ★ Dawn
Polarity ★ Male, positive
Exhortation ★ To *will*
Musical Instruments ★ Wind instruments, harp
Colours ★ Gold, white
Season ★ Spring
Magical Instrument ★ Wand
Altar Symbol ★ Incense
Communion Symbol ★ Scent
Archangel ★ Raphael
Human Senses ★ Hearing, smell

Art Forms ★ Poetry Painting
Animals ★ Birds, bats
Mythical Beast ★ Winged horse
Magical Arts ★ Divinations
Guide Forms ★ Sky/weather gods
Meditation ★ Sky, clouds
Images & Themes ★ Mountain tops, flying, sunrise, wisdom and knowledge

HOW YOU CAN GET IN TOUCH WITH YOUR AIR ENERGY

"When we are present with and summon the magic of Air, we gain wings"

★ Use Air energy when making wishes around the following: Travel, exam success and study, job interviews, meditation, relaxation, more effective communication with others, improved expression and articulation of needs, mental stability, increasing knowledge-base, nervous stress relief

★ In magical practices, Air can be represented by smoke, which can be created by burning a joss stick or incense. The following tools and methods can also be used to carry your dreams to the skies and ether: Feathers, hanging mobiles in the breeze with your wishes attached, paper darts, autumn leaves, and airborne seeds

★ The best days on which to employ Air magic are Wednesdays, ruled by the planet of communication Mercury, or Thursdays, ruled by Thor, the Norse god of thunder. If possible, choosing a windy day with gales or thunderstorms will make your work more powerful. Air spells are also most effective when performed beneath an open sky; a high mountain would be an ideal location. Writing a wish on a kite or a balloon and guiding it through the air, as high as possible, by a piece of string can harness the magic of the Air spirits, who will help you clarify and manifest your desires, through quite literally releasing your wish into the wind

★ Spend time in open, fresh, clean air regularly

★ Spend time in wide open spaces and engage in outdoor activities that make use of the air around you, such as flying a kite or ballooning

★ Learn Prana-, Chi- or Ki-related disciplines, martial arts, meditation and yoga that focus on breathing, focus, mental-detachment and concentration

★ Read as much as you can; be an eternal student

★ Blue-coloured crystals will activate your connection with the element of Air and enhance your dreams, soothe your fears, calm your nervous system, help you communicate, bring about inner peace, and assist in self-transformation

★ Develop your networking skills

★ Throw intellectual dinner parties

★ Join a discussion group or an online Internet chat room

★ Practice deep breathing

★ Learn about meteorology, cloud formations, the atmosphere and the weather

★ Use a negative ion machine, humidifier or air purifier in your home

★ Don't smoke, or if you do, quit (being associated with the lungs, Geminis should particularly take note of this)

★ Sleep on an air mattress

★ Meditate on the Swords suit in the Tarot (the Swords suit represents the Air element)

★ Take a course - in anything and everything!

★ Know a little bit about everything; trivia is more powerful than its given credit for!

★ Write; keep a journal

★ Visit the library on a regular basis; join a book discussion group

★ Look after your lungs, other components of your respiratory system, and your nervous system

★ Take a course, learn a language, or otherwise make a commitment to a learning activity which requires discipline, focus and mental energy

★ Take a course on improving your relationships

★ Hire a jumping castle and invite your friends over!

★ Jump on a trampoline

★ Practice public speaking often, even solo in front of a mirror

★ Forget your mind chatter and allow your heart to lead occasionally; it always knows where to go

★ When working with the Air element in magical practice, stand at the East quarter of your magical space, as the East is its domain, and invite its living essence into your 'circle'

★ Air spirits are also known as air devas, zephyrs, builders or sylphs, and can be called upon to calm our nerves, cleanse our thoughts, clear anxiety and fear, and to help us focus with greater mental clarity, so Air signs would be wise to adopt one (or all) as their very own spirit guide!

YOUR MODE ★ CARDINAL

Each sign belongs to one of the three quadruplicities, Cardinal, Fixed and Mutable. If we closely examine the Earth's yearly cycle, we can form a very accurate picture of the nature of these quadruplicities, for they correspond directly with the manifestation of the seasons. Each season has three months: the first month brings the new phase of the cycle, the second month brings a concentration of the season's energy to its fullest expression, and the third month represents the transition from the current season to the next one. The astrological quadruplicities represent the three basic qualities in all life: creation (Cardinal), perseveration (Fixed) and destruction (Mutable). Every thing that is born, from a period of time to a human being, experiences a life and then dies. In this context, death can be taken to mean that the form of the energy changes; but the energy itself can never be annihilated, for form is mortal, whereas essence is immortal.

The Cardinal mode covers the signs Aries, Cancer, Libra and Capricorn, and is the most initiating and self-motivated group of the three modes, able to instigate and inspire beginnings; in other words, to "get the ball rolling." The Cardinal mode has an initiating action and quality, operating with ambition, enthusiasm, independence and enterprise. Forceful, opportunistic, and at times aggressive, you have the will to accomplish and creatively project yourself onto the world. You charge right in to get the job done - but you can fail just as spectacularly. Although you have a great start-up ability, tenacity and endurance are not your fortes, and you often don't follow things through to the end. If there is no crisis for you to tackle, you may even make one up just to create a challenge for yourself. You find it hard to be held under anyone's thumb and will always find a way to wriggle free to set off on your next quest. Your energies may be directed towards yourself, your home and family, or the wider world of career or society, but in any case it is difficult to divert your attention away from your chosen course. Cardinal signs have great drive, are self-motivated and would rather lead than follow. It is hard to influence you because you make your own firm decisions and believe that you know best. The Cardinal mode signifies beginnings, decision-making, boldness, courage, will, new starts, and initiations. You tend to be dynamic, authoritative, 'bossy', active, restless, involved, busy and energetic, and are determined initiators of goals and new purposes. The Sun's entry into the Cardinal signs indicates the beginning of seasons in the northern hemisphere: the start of Aries marks the Spring Equinox, the beginning of Libra the Autumn Equinox, the start of Cancer the Winter Solstice, and the beginning of Capricorn the Summer Solstice.

Libra is the most easy going sign of the Cardinal quality; you will use language, charm and your sociable, amiable nature to get things started, and people will usually follow your graceful lead.

YOUR RULING PLANET ★ VENUS

The Lover, Charmer, Seducer, Romantic & Artist

Planetary Meditation
I am my Earth (my body),
and my Sky (my transcendence)
I am my Sun (my spirit),
and my Moon (my soul)
I am my Venus (my pleasure),
and my Jupiter (my faith)
I am my Mars (my courage),
and my Saturn (my lessons)
I am my Mercury (my thoughts),
and my Uranus (my truth)
I am my Neptune (my dreams),
and my Pluto (my transformation)

Each planet has its own distinctive and original meaning which, according to its position in the zodiac, combines with the qualities that are inherent in each of the twelve astrological signs. If a planet is your sign's ruler, however, it exerts a significant influence upon your life, regardless of its birth chart or zodiacal position.

Benefic ★ Love, Beauty, Harmony, Unison, Pleasure
★ 225 Day Cycle

★ KEY WORDS ★
Love, Beauty, Art, Harmony, Affection, Desire, Relating, Relationships, Pleasure, Acceptance, Social Graces, Vanity, Sociability, Persuasion, Luxury, Unison, Aesthetics,

Outward Style, Indulgence, Refinement, Values, Comfort, Resources, Enjoyment, Agreeableness, Good Humour, Symmetry, Proportion, Mutuality, Sympathy

★ KEY CONCEPTS ★
★ Love, Relating, Harmony ★
★ Beauty in Form ★
★ Social Orientation ★
★ Refinement of Artistic Tastes ★
★ Values & Priorities ★
★ Leisure, Pleasure, Music, Art ★
★ Sentiments in Love & Sharing ★
★ Sensual Enjoyment ★
★ Ostentation & Luxury ★
★ Emotions Connected to Love & Possessions ★
★ Justice & Fair Play ★

Day ★ Friday

Number ★ 6

Basic Energy & Magic ★ Love, Sociability

Colours ★ Light Blue, Green, Pink, Soft Yellow, Pastels

Gods/Goddesses/Angel ★ Aphrodite, Venus, Raphael

Metals ★ Copper, Bronze, Brass

Gems/Minerals ★ Jade, Lapis Lazuli, Rose Quartz, Emerald, Kunzite, Peridot, Malachite (Copper Ore), Sapphire, Green Aventurine

Trees/Shrubs ★ Peach, Pear, Alder, Ash, Birch, Cypress, Fig, Almond

Flowers/Fruits/Herbs ★ Rose, Carnation, Lilac, Pomegranate, Apple

Wood ★ Sycamore

Fabric ★ Satin

Animal ★ Cat, Dove, Sparrow

Element ★ Air

Zodiacal Signs ★ Taurus, Libra

Zodiacal Influences ★ Rules Libra and Taurus; Exalted in Pisces; Detriment Aries; Fall Virgo

"Venus is a woman. At her best, she is what every mortal female might aspire to become and every male to have as his mate. She is capable of any depth of understanding, every height of love. She is the ultimate in beauty of spirit as well as of body. She can show any tenderness, any strength in expressing her love."
***Astrology for Skeptics (sic)*, Charlotte MacLeod, 1972**

Venus was one of the five planets known in ancient times. Discovered by the Babylonians in about 3000 B.C., Venus also appears in the astronomical records of several other old civilisations. Venus or Aphrodite as she is sometimes referred to, was said to have sprung from the seed of Uranus and to have risen naked from the foaming water of the sea, as in Botticelli's famous painting *The Birth of Venus*.

The glyph (or symbol) for Venus is a circle with a cross underneath it, the symbol for the female, and it connotes spirit (the circle) over matter (the cross). Without the crescent of soul of consciousness, Venus is objective. This glyph is related to the Egyptian life-giving symbol, the Ankh, representing the 'mirror' of Venus reflecting our attitudes and values, and is also the biological symbol for female. This image is quintessentially Venus, with its strong associations with grace, desire, luxury, femininity, adornment, love, beauty and harmony.

Venus, named in honour of the goddess of love Aphrodite, is concerned with our relationships and the choices we make in life, both personal and material. It influences the decisions we make, especially when it comes to deciding upon the things and people we value. The mythic Venus or Aphrodite brought fertility, birth, love and passions to all she touched, and through her craftsman husband Hephaestus, she influenced the creation of beautiful objects. She teaches us that contentment and satisfaction are found in nature, in creating and sharing sensual delights, and in giving and receiving affection.

Venus is the secondary feminine principle in our natal chart, the 'female within'. It relates to our urge for relationships, attraction, sensual pleasures, social activities, our sense of beauty, our self-esteem and self-value. It can enhance self-confidence, therefore not only encouraging the *giving* of love, but the *receiving* of it too.

Venus is the planet of love, beauty and pleasure. The signs in which it falls in your birth chart will determine how you express affection and appreciate beauty, and show the sort of relationships and people you attract, as well as your behaviour in love. In a male's birth chart, the position of Venus, a feminine archetype, reveals what he typically projects onto the women he encounters, what he is attracted to in a partner, the qualities he seeks, and what he desires and is turned on by. Venus is his idealised picture of the feminine, his anima, his ideal woman. Venus in a female's birth chart describes a woman's femininity, her image of herself (the hand-mirror), how she presents herself to the world, her desire to look good, what she values in herself and how comfortable she feels with her feminine side. While this is not always true, it reflects how most individuals operate, particularly before one has reached the level of maturity or self-awareness that brings a person to a more balanced inner centre. Perhaps it is an overused cliché, but we cannot receive love from another until we truly love ourselves. There is truth in this concept, and the astrological examination of the planet Venus in one's chart provides the best mirror for this truth.

Venus represents our urge for relationships, artistic expression and tastes, sensual pleasures and that nature of our social connections. It is also about relating, harmony and our sense of values. It shows us how we give and receive, appreciate, and merge with others. While Venus and Mars are the feminine and masculine elements of a chart respectively, this is an oversimplification: desire is the province of Mars, attraction of Venus. Where desire seeks to acquire its object, love seeks to attract it. Venus does not need to exert much effort to attract the things she loves and values; she simply magnetises them to her. however, she invariably always operates in concert with Mars when she sets her heart on something or someone. What Venus wishes for, Mars sets off to attain and conquer for her.

Venus influences our feelings and motivations, and governs our more outer emotional selves. Whether you regard the planets as springs of cosmic activity or as symbols, the astrological importance of Venus is easy to understand. It is commonly known as the *planet of love*, which is an over-simplification, but it does have a powerful effect on our feelings, desires and what we are drawn towards. It also governs how we relate to other people socially and economically and has an influence on our attitude to money and possessions.

Venus is never more than 48 degrees from the Sun, so it either occupies the same sign in a birth chart as the Sun, or falls within two signs either side of it. When it is possible to see Venus, only during the three hours before sunrise or three hours after sunset, it is the most brilliant object in the sky other than the Sun and the Moon. Living up to its reputation for beauty and symmetry, Venus is a perfect sphere, unlike the other planets which are flattened somewhat at their poles. Through telescopes her surface appears serenely smooth, and she has the least eccentric orbit of all the bodies.

Otherwise known as the Morning Star or Evening Star, depending on her position in the cosmos and her relationship with the Sun, Venus can tell us about the type of love we give to someone special. It has been theorised that when one is born with Venus as the Morning Star, she is more untamed, primary, sexual and instinctive in her romantic expressions, and tends to be more impulsive in relationships; they fall in love quickly and without much reflection. When Venus is the Evening Star in one's chart, there is a greater maturity in her gift of love, a greater concern with relationship as opposed to fun and romance. Those born with an Evening Star Venus are not necessarily more successful in partnerships, but their awareness and reflections on love as a deeper transformational process undoubtedly adds a more solid dimension to it.

Venus tells us a lot about how we give and receive affection. In our chart she shows us our socialisation and development, and our relationship patterns/formation style. Its sign is an indication of the qualities that we find attractive and value, whether in another person, a philosophy, an art piece or a landscape. It also signifies our projections in relationships, and the qualities we admire in others. Ultimately, Venus tells us about our urge to love, appreciate and relate, and merge with others.

This beautiful planet is all about appreciation, equality and fairness, our sense of values, aesthetics, our likes and dislikes, and our tastes. She plays a role in our creativity, as she is closely linked with what repels or attracts us, and motivates us to 'create' and artistically express accordingly.

Finances and resources are also ruled by Venus, and she governs money and gifts, as well as sensuous indulgences, such as fine wines, jewellery, gourmet foods, fancy adornments, imported chocolates, perfumes, music and painting. There is indeed a decorative quality about Venus, as well as a feeling of abundance and luxury. As well as opulence and the good life, Venus is associated with fertility, creation and reproduction (her influence coupled with the Moon). Hence the purpose of Venus is to bestow creativity and new life. On another level still, Venus is said to add depth to friendships, strengthen bonds between a child and a parent, and to bring popularity to rulers.

People with a strong Venus in their chart, such as those with a Taurus or Libra Sun, Moon or Ascendant, are social, graceful and friendly, superficial and light-hearted, love pleasurable social pursuits, need others to feel balanced and 'complete', have a well-developed sense of aesthetic awareness, and express affection with ease and grace. They can be the 'hostess with the mostest', possessing all the delightful attributes that make friendships amiable and satisfying as long as the harsher realities of everyday life are kept at bay.

Venus is essentially fruitful and feminine like the Moon. Both rule the gentler and finer emotions of both genders. On their own, they are inclined to be vacillating and lacking in direction and discipline, but given the support of more purposeful influences from other planets in the horoscope, Venusian accomplishments are often wonderful and always artistically pleasing. Venus is known as the 'lesser benefic' after Jupiter, the 'higher benefic', with Venus being more material and physical than her moralistic, loftier counterpart.

Our inner Venus is the part of us that moves to bridge the gap again after a conflict, and has to do with mediating, negotiating and resolution. Too much Venusian influence can result in over-indulgence, superficiality, greed, over-emphasis on materiality, insincerity and promiscuity. These negative tendencies may manifest in destructive ways, unless we can learn to 'allow relationships into our lives rather than taking our lives into our relationships'. It has been said that while women are more likely to project Mars in relationships, men are more likely to project Venus in relationships.

Because Venus rules over two zodiac signs, Taurus and Libra, and both are essentially different (Taurus being Fixed, Libra being Cardinal for one thing), it manifests itself in different ways in each sign: in Taurus pleasure can be found in the Earthly pleasures of material comforts, while in Libra it comes out as a more intellectual approach to beauty, perhaps chic and elegant. Venus's influence in the Libran realm is also more concerned with the interplay of opposites that exist in relationships, and bringing these polarities into harmony. Many astrologers and psychoanalysts believe that we are often magnetised by precisely those qualities that we lack in ourselves, and that we subconsciously choose to incorporate those absent characteristics into ourselves by becoming immersed in them through the medium of a partner who embodies them. However, many people forget why they 'attracted' such a partner in the first place, and then attempt to transform that person into a clone of themselves, or perhaps into a projected idealised image.

Venus is concerned with people's principal desires: love and money. She facilitates harmony between people, connection to luxuries and is generally the planet of good times. She is said to be concerned with our relationships, our values, and the choices we make in life, both personal and material. Venus is happiest when giving of herself as well as receiving affection from others, as she loves to relate, and strives for emotional satisfaction and nourishment. Taurus's energy gives her a sensual edge, Libra's energy gives her an intellectual, sharing and sociable edge. Marriage falls under the dominion of Libra, while the more mundane, practical aspects of Earth life such as food, nourishment, shelter and home, are attributed to Taurus. In Taurus, she shows us our ability to prosper in the material sense, describing how we acquire, use and conserve our resources. In Libra, she lends an energy of social grace, physical attractiveness, and the apparently effortless ability to enjoy good relationships with the opposite sex. However, the downside of Venus in both signs is that you may be inherit her less desirable characteristics, which are self-indulgence, vanity, hedonism, insincerity, low self-worth, superficiality, gluttony, promiscuity (the word 'venereal', pertaining to sexually transmitted infections, is derived from Venus), or being emotionally demanding in your relationships.

Associated with the things we hold dear to us, Venus is intrinsically linked with sensuality and in short, anything that appeals to the senses, which could include anything from music, art, dancing and movies, to food, sex, exercise and anything else that feels good or enlivens our senses somehow. Because we can be very attached to the things we possess or enjoy, Venus will tell us what we will fight to keep.

Although it is well-known that Venus rules our style of 'give and take' in partnerships, she also has a need to be constantly validated by others to know that she *is* really beautiful and lovely and lovable; after all, she is strongly tied up in our self-worth and value systems - how we value ourselves falling under this umbrella. Generally, Venus in the horoscope addresses issues of self-esteem and how our self-worth holds up or interacts in relationships. One can analyse what makes people fall in love by observing their Venus position, and also what kind of validation or assurance they need from others to bring about their own inner love.

Venus is associated with the pentagram *, gifts, dressmakers, polite, sociable, colour, Friday, holidays, rings, present, cakes, festivities, gentle, music, attractive, flirting, comforts, social affairs, banquets, weddings, duets, caresses, ribbons, adornment, decorations, beauty, honey, money, girls, singing, society, cash, fancy goods, poise, alliances, popular, coalitions, friendship, courtship, ease, gentility, wallets, fashion models, bracelets, lingerie, companions, relaxation, possessions, arbitration, glamour, gains, comrades, candy, mates, boutiques, florists, décor, gloves, good taste, donations, beauticians, wages, gems, social gatherings, concerts, finance, millinery, romance, costumes, pleasure, gowns, grace, leisure, beauty parlours, profits, equality, blossoms, fun, calm, matchmaking, symmetry, flattery, peace, gratitude, sex appeal, bouquets, marriage proposals, greetings, clothes, ladies, sweets, vases, garnishing, rouge, refinement, elegance, etiquette, garments, delicacies, negotiation, cooperation, entertainment, cosmetics, garlands, serenades, flowers, amusement, art, seashells, finery, artists, melody, truces, wigs, brooches, honeymoons, drapes, fiancé, hairdressers, lace, favours, luxury, decorators, pastels, receptions, parties, reconciliation, hairstyles, marriage, songs, oysters, happiness, bonnets, fraternities, sweethearts, embroidery, harmony, celebrations, hats, necklaces, recreation, style, partners, culture, hospitality, toiletries, good manners, confectioners, ornaments, cabarets, affection, pacifists, scarves, emotional attachments, kindness, ballet, diplomacy, dresses, charm, gaiety, furnishings, paintings, fine arts, femininity, tapestries, enjoyment, kidneys, romantic engagements, love, dolls, emeralds, salons, copper, income, interior decorators, intimacy, jewellery, social invitations, lockets, makeup, sugar, orchestras, pacts, suitors, tact and women. I'm sure you get the idea!

This Venusian energy and influence, throughout your whole life, gives Librans the gifts of grace, equability, an easy going nature, charm, accommodating to others' needs, cooperation, affection, tact, kindness, friendliness, refinement, appreciation for beauty, aesthetic awareness and placidity. Too much of this Venusian energy can make one vain, lazy, indecisive, weak-willed, dependent, careless, impractical, promiscuous, manipulative, possessive, overly romantic, self-indulgent and greedy. But the Venus-inspired Libran always knows what keeps his soul in perfect harmony; after all, your motto is "I Balance," because deep down, you fear being out of kilter in any area of life regarding relationships, money and overall comfort. How will *you* use your phenomenally powerful Venusian influence?

* The 'Pentagram of Venus' ★ The pentagram, a five-pointed star, is an ancient and arcane symbol having numerous meanings. Its origins are obscure, but it is interesting to note that in Ancient Egypt all stars were depicted with five points, and one possibility for this is the pentagram's relationship with the planet Venus: the astronomers of the day noticed that every eight years the planet's movements completed the drawing of a pentagram in the sky.

YOUR HOUSE IN THE HOROSCOPE ★ THE SEVENTH HOUSE

DESCENDANT - DESC - Cusp of the Seventh House. This is the degree of the zodiac rising on the western horizon at the moment of our birth. It is the point of awareness of others: "How I Relate to an Other."

The Seventh House deals with your closest and most intimate relationships, those on a personal basis and in a marriage or similar situation. Close professional partnerships and associations, as well as more hostile and competitive forces such as open enemies, are also indicated.

A house is one of the twelve sections dividing the terrestrial globe, viewed from a precise time and geographical place, into sectors from the poles to the horizon. The horoscope, or birth chart, is divided into these twelve sections called houses. Each house governs a different area or 'department' of life, such as relationships, career, leisure and even karma. The reason for this division of the Earth into houses can be understood when we consider that the Sun's rays affect us differently in the morning, at noon and at night, and also in summer and winter, and if we study the cause, we will readily observe that it is the angle at which the ray strikes us or the Earth which produces that difference in effect. Similarly, with the stellar rays, astrologers have observed that a child born at or near midday, when the Sun's rays strike the birthplace from the Tenth House, has an improved chance of public or career advancement in life than one born after sunset. By similar observations and tabulations, it has been found that the other planetary rays affect the various departments of life when their ray is projected through the other houses, and therefore each house is said to 'rule' or govern certain departments of the human life experience.

The Seventh House, ruled by Libra, is the house of marriage, partnerships and close relationships with others. As an Air sign, this is one of the three houses of relationships, and is an all-important 'angular' House, being the Descendant, meaning that it forms one of the four significant angles of the birth chart (the other three being the First House or Ascendant, the Fourth House or Imum Coeli, and the Tenth House or Midheaven). But where Gemini is concerned with relationships on a personal level and Aquarius with relationships on a transpersonal or wider-reaching level, Libra and the Seventh House are primarily linked with relationships on an interpersonal level, that is, through relating and dealing with others.

The Seventh House is otherwise known as the House of Marriage, and is all about partnerships. This can be partnerships in a business sense, a marriage or a committed relationship. Other exoteric and esoteric keywords for the Seventh House include: Long-term associations, open enemies, the animus, and the relationship between the soul and personality.

The Seventh House is often, and most aptly, called the House of Relationships. As such, it describes your interactions with other people, how others regard you, your awareness of and dealings with others, our open enemies and adversaries, how we select our partners, and significantly, the types of relationships and partners we seek and attract. It reveals the significant other in our life, what we need most from them, and the rapport that develops between the two of you. As the Descendant (directly opposite the projected self of the Ascendant), it indicates the qualities we unconsciously look for in others and what we magnetise, our anima or animus, our 'shadow', what is foreign to us (e.g. the opposite sex), and what is unknown, foreign territory. It also reveals our attitudes towards close relationship and our ability to get along with and cooperate with others. It is also associated with agreements, contracts, dealings with the public, opponents, competitors and open enemies.

Often we are subconsciously attracted to those who carry a strong emphasis of the sign on the cusp of our own birth chart's Seventh House. Your 'shadow' self can indeed be reflected by your partner, as we tend to marry our own shadow, something we may not be conscious of or recognise in ourselves. This is usually the result of projecting ourselves onto others - personal projection is a matter of the First House, and any projections are directed outwards and onto those closest to us. The Seventh House, being the First House's direct opposite, is the recipient of this process. The process of being able to recognise our own qualities in another, things we can't always access in ourselves, encapsulates the essence of the Seventh House, and the qualities of this house desire expression in one-to-one relationships.

The Seventh House, on a more mundane level, is connected with cooperation, joint undertakings, healthy competition, everyone we approach as an equal, mutuality, and also rules any significant contractual undertaking between two people, mostly in marriage or business. Because this house encompasses dealings with others in general, it can also include hostilities and conflicts. It suggests who our open (known) enemies may be, the nature of any relationship discord or harmony you are likely to encounter, the manner in which you relate to those closest to you, and also the way you see them.

As well as affairs of committed love and marriage, close friends, business associates/partners, and known enemies or competition, this house also deals with negotiations, mutual interests, and any legal matters arising from broken partnerships or legal contracts such as separation, divorce or marital discord.

YOUR OPPOSITE SIGN ★ ARIES
WHAT YOU CAN LEARN FROM THE RAM

If we look at the zodiac, we can see that it can be broadly divided into two hemispheres, this division being based on the natural division of the year by the two equinoxes. Astrologers often refer to the first six signs, the hemisphere in which the day predominates (the days being longer in the spring and summer months), as the Personal Sphere of Experience, and the second six signs, the hemisphere in which nights are longer, as the Social Sphere of Experience. These two halves of the zodiac perfectly balance and complement each other, and each individual 'personal' zodiac sign has something to teach its directly opposite 'social' zodiac sign. To generalise, the signs of the personal sphere tend to experience life through a type of self-projection and self-interest which is often socially uncomplicated, unsophisticated or naïve. Their objective is to learn greater social awareness and thereby integrate themselves with the larger, more Universal human collective. On the other hand, the signs of the social sphere are prone to experience life through the use of their more developed social consciousness. In essence, the personal signs (Aries, Taurus, Gemini, Cancer, Leo, Virgo) usually provide stimulation and new energy to their environment, while the social, more Universal signs (Libra, Scorpio, Sagittarius, Capricorn, Aquarius, Pisces) provide experience, opportunities for wider expression, and give a more broad-minded approach and perspective to their surroundings.

Each sign in a pair seeks and is attracted to the qualities of its complementary opposing sign. Aries seeks the balanced judgement and the consideration of others of Libra; Libra desires to have more of the self-direction and independence of Aries. Aries dwells within the realm of self-projection through *individual* impulse, while Libra resides within the realm of self-projection through *social* impulse.

Although the word 'opposite' conjures up feelings of separateness and differences, the astrological polarities should not be seen as two signs in conflict with each other - their positive expression is to create a natural balance and equilibrium. Each sign has something to learn from its opposite, but also has a contribution to make towards the other sign's more evolved expression. The First (Aries) and Seventh (Libra) House polarity is concerned with awareness of *self* versus awareness of *others*.

The First and Seventh Houses, as complementary opposites, show your individual self-image and how you relate in close contact with other people. In any personal relationship (Seventh House), you will be seeking qualities (consciously or unconsciously) which will complement your own personality (First House) or which are needed to fill some psychological gap in your character. The signs and planets connected with these houses will show what these qualities are.

Positive and Cardinal, the polarity of Libra and Aries in some ways epitomises the battle of the sexes. Venus seeks union and acts thoughtfully, Mars acts independently and on impulse, but as with relationships between male and female, each needs the other. The strong individuality of Aries needs to learn the balance and cooperation offered by Libra. Indeed, self-orientation and the desire for freedom can mellow through the experience of compromise in a relationship with another person. But Libra's social involvement and its feeling of loss that exists without the 'other half' aspect inherent in any partnership, may lead to uncertainty and dependence. Libra is gently strengthened if it can develop the qualities of initiative, greater independence, and single-mindedness characterised by the self-interested and ego-driven Aries.

The bold, assertive, self-centred individual (Aries) seeks to become aware of others, and to develop a capacity for objective cooperation with them in relationships (Libra). And the rational, measured and reasonable individual, adept at compromise and cooperation (Libra) seeks to develop a capacity for initiative, self-assertion and independence.

With Aries as your complementary oppositional teacher, yours is a quest to become assertive and self-empowered. You have a tendency to be indecisive, always considering the needs of others first. You need to discover a clearer sense of your own identity and initiate your own projects.

Aries relates to confidence, impulse, raw instincts, and a pressing desire to follow one's own path. Libra's lessons come by learning that true success comes through becoming more aware of the *self* and to initiate more things, more often and with more confidence; to be spontaneous without ignoring the needs of others; in essence, to put the *self first* for a change. You will realise that you can be a much happier, whole and harmonious person if you do this, and will be a greater help to others, which is of utmost importance to you - being there for others, and in particular, keeping your relationships on an even keel. Taking some time out for yourself on a regular basis is one strategy you can easily use to enhance your partnerships, as you will find yourself in a better headspace to enable you to give more. Because, as you become increasingly aware of your own needs and asserting them, you are better equipped to recognise, respond to, and ultimately satisfy the needs of others. By truly being yourself and exuding your unique energy, rather than what you think others expect from you, you will attract happier and more satisfying interactions and connections with others.

As a typical Libra, you prioritise a balanced lifestyle and harmonious relationships, but may need to appease your equally strong, albeit somewhat suppressed, desire for excitement, in order for your soul to flourish. Your insecurity about your own personal identity, and perhaps an ego which has merged with and pleased others too much in the past, has led you to become overly dependent on other people in your seeking of wellbeing and fulfilment. Often this only leads to disappointment, as you drive the other person away with your intense neediness and over-eagerness to compromise for peace's sake. Working on strengthening your ego and self-confidence, and putting yourself first without being selfish, are your keys to soul development. Once you have formed a relationship which is balanced and ego-less from both sides, your natural need for passion and freedom will assert itself, and your relationships will be a lot healthier and satisfying.

Learning the wisdom of the Ram will enable you to conquer indecision and to select one course of action rather than sitting on the fence considering alternatives, and consequently getting nowhere fast - or *ever*. You need to work on developing a stronger sense of self that is separate from others, and your contact with your needs and desires will help you to really go after what you want in life, to take greater initiative, to act independently, and to find pleasure in your activities on your own so that you are not so dependent on sharing with others for sustenance.

You need to invoke more enthusiasm, spark and zest for life, and this in turn will enliven your relationships and enable you to enjoy social interactions without fear or insecurities, and strengthen your bonds. Rather than avoiding conflict, by developing your confidence and self-assertion, you will confront it head on and be more effective in finding your true individual place in the scheme of things. Once you are able to bring a stronger sense of your identity into personal encounters, you enter into relationships as an autonomous individual, and are therefore able to grow relationships that promote your soul's growth rather than catering to your weaknesses and inability to stand on your own, which only reinforces those undesirable behaviours.

If you are typical of the Scales, you are probably over-developed in the following areas: dependence on others for your happiness; searching outside of yourself for enchantment; overly relationship-oriented and focused; striving for equality, justice and fairness, often at a personal cost; fruitless searching for your soul mate or 'other' half; cooperating with, accommodating for and developing committed and mutually satisfying relationships; being too law-abiding and appeasing; pleasing others and attempting to be liked; over-awareness and care for others' points of view; weak convictions; giving insincere flattery; lethargic, 'paralysed' and placid; trying to cultivate loving relationships but going about it in the wrong ways, for example by being smothering or demanding; fear of self or others; lack of courage; weighing up alternatives, over-evaluating situations, delaying action, indecisiveness; fence-sitting; striving for balance, peace and harmony, mediating and generally avoiding conflict at all costs.

This psychological journey from a Libran-themed character to an Aries-flavoured spirit, is not always an easy pill to swallow; Aries's abrasiveness can scratch the gentle, delicate Libran's nature. By nature, you are an individual who needs to live in harmony within an intimate social circle and only feel at ease when you are appreciated, comforted and supported. Aries teaches you that you need to develop a much stronger sense of self and your place in the world. Libra tends to define himself by his place in the world, not his opinion of him*self*, and because of this he is often inclined to make excessive concessions in order to keep peace with others, since he prefers to avoid struggles and confrontations at all costs. Circumstances work well if you learn how to assert yourself more fully as an individual with your own personality, convictions, opinions, ideas and tastes, not just those borrowed from others. Sometimes you may need to lead rather than join in, and this may involve some decidedly uncomfortable (for you) impositions of your choices and decisions upon other people.

Obstacles and challenges are really just strategically placed hurdles that are meant to remind us of our inner strength and courage. Therefore, as long as you remember to hold tight to the wilful power that your Aries teacher advises you to cultivate and nurture, you will flourish, grow, evolve and generally have a firmer direction in life.

Having outlined the characteristics, you need to outgrow, and the characteristics you need to develop and incorporate into your life, you should additionally seek out and surround yourself with the people and symbols that will support your journey. By surrounding yourself with people who understand, and symbols that exude this Arien energy, you are ensuring your own destiny by keeping your soul's mission and path to fulfilment consistently around you.

Catering to the needs of others is over-developed in your character. You are the quintessential people-pleaser and charmer who has over-compromised to the detriment of truly growing your true *self*. Recognising this and working on your ego strength and *true* essence, will help your soul greatly along its ultimate life path.

WHAT THE RAM CAN ULTIMATELY TEACH THE SCALES

Release ★ Indecisiveness, co-dependency, uncertainty, easily-led temperament, lack of firmness, insincere charm, agreeableness, fear of conflicts, appeasing behaviours, pleasing everyone but yourself, complete selflessness, obsessive attachments to justice and fairness, over-reliance on harmony and balance, 'tit for that' mentality, narcissism

Embrace ★ Some healthy selfishness, finding yourself, strong identity, audacity, fighting spirit, power of action, adventure, boldness, courage, assertiveness, direction, purpose, independence, confronting conflicts, incisiveness, self-confidence, initiative, sincerity, self-awareness, trusting your impulses, moderation and discrimination in who and what you give your energy to, and a healthy ego

Your complementary opposite sign Aries is action-orientated, self-directed, self-centred, assertive, frank, direct, outspoken, energetic, sexual, passionate, competitive, initiating, impulsive, quick, subjective, aware of own point of view, seeks excitement, satisfies own desires, maintains personal liberty and provokes conflict. On the other end of the scale, Libra relates to the success that comes mainly through cooperating with others. The Scales also relate to indecisiveness, co-dependency and agreeableness which can come across as insincere.

There is a certain laziness and dullness that manifests in the Libran character as a result of years, perhaps decades, of allowing yourself to be pushed by other people or circumstances into situations that spark smouldering resentment which, when it has festered for too long, can make you feel that life is futile and empty. You may have allowed yourself to be trapped in a relationship or societal contexts that have created undesirable states of being whereby you become more vulnerable to being drained by others; and so the cycle repeats - until you learn that there *is* a more dynamic destiny you are fated for through developing that *stronger, more decisive sense of self*. If you only take one lesson away from your Aries teacher, let this one be it.

You need to work on the following for your soul to evolve and flourish (Aries-themed concepts): Action-orientate yourself; self-direction; trusting in yourself rather than relying on others opinions of yourself; engaging in healthy competition; creating and maintaining a sense of personal freedom; intensity, energy, frankness, becoming more direct and outspoken; developing impulsivity and a youthful outlook; becoming subjective and more aware of your own points of view; courage in your convictions; firmness and confidence in your life's direction; provoking healthy conflict and incorporating more excitement into your life; developing your sexual side and expressing yourself more passionately; pleasing yourself and satisfying your own desires.

Magnum opus is Latin for the 'great work' and is how the alchemists refer to creation. The prime alchemical pursuit was not only to transmute lead into gold, but to transform the self, to transmute one's essence and become a 'denizen of the Universe' and a co-creator in the Great Work. Fire was of prime importance in the alchemical process, and it is no coincidence that your best teacher Aries, is of the Fire element. The inner Fire the Ram embodies can be seen as far more efficacious than that gained through the outer plane or through external relationships. To the Arian spirit and the true alchemist alike, there is no higher pursuit than the continual burning of that inner Fire. The Libran soul needs only to tend to this inner self, stoke the embers and watch the sparks fly and the flames grow. In perhaps simpler language, the power of your inner Fire needs to find appropriate expression in your life.

To evolve to your fullest potential, Aries can assist your journey greatly by imparting his lessons of self-confidence, courage, spontaneity, ego strength, leadership, putting yourself first, leaps of faith, naïve charm, and above all, true boldness. Your life's path can only be enriched by this sharing it with your awe-inspiring, wonder-filled Arian friend. You will find that you will transform swiftly from graceful charmer to courageous champion in no time at all once you make the firm decision to do so. After all, Aries, more than any other sign, knows that fortune favours the bold!

MAGIC, DRAWING, ATTRACTION, SPELLS, RITUALS, WISHING & POWER

A Note on the Universe

Within each of us resides the merging of the Sun and the Moon, the dance of the constellations, the vibrations of the planets, and the vast microcosm and macrocosm of the entire *Universe*. Uni means 'one' and Verse means 'song'; therefore, the word Universe literally means 'One Song'. If you learn to tune yourself in, you can even hear it!

What is Magic?

Magic is a kind of special energy that is beyond description, and like most kinds of energy it has its own rules and ways of being manipulated. It remains an elusive term, and no definition has ever really found Universal acceptance. Attempts to separate it from superstition, religion and other-worldly phenomena on the one hand, and 'science' on the other, are ridden with difficulties. However slippery the term 'magic' might be, there is a general agreement that most of us wish for more of its presence in our lives and often fall short of achieving this wish.

Those performing spells, 'asking the Universe', wishing, praying, or undertaking rituals, are using this very special energy to draw things to them. Learning to manipulate energy in these ways is never hard (and shouldn't be), but it can be complex and does require knowledge, practice, creativity, patience and above all, imagination. Most of us use simple magic every day, whether by saying little prayers, making wishes, visualising, and exchanging - sending out and receiving - good, positive or hopeful vibes. When you understand that all the forces and magic you need are *within* you, and you learn to *believe* in that power, you are then able to make all manner of changes to your life and, most importantly, yourself.

Magic is an invisible force which connects and permeates everything. Every thought you have and every action you take, will affect the strength of this force, and can be influenced and directed towards a specific purpose by using certain means. The most important of these are your intentions, facing in the direction of your desired outcome, your will and your *belief* that it works. The more you want something to happen, and the clearer you can visualise the desired outcome, the stronger your will and feelings towards it will be, ensuring an avalanche of amazing people, events and circumstances will flow into your experiences, gathering speed, momentum and power as it nears your goal or dream.

The Universe (or whichever higher power you believe in) works for us and through us. Ideas are given to us but they must be carried out *through* us, in the form of asking or acting or performing a ritual or casting a specific spell. The Universe's abundance is your abundance, and it flows through your mind into manifestation. The Universe or Divine Being in which you believe, gives you the necessary ideas and clothes them with all that is needed to bring them into form when we ask *believing*.

Based on ancient human beliefs, systems and superstitions, declaring what you want and acting out your deepest desires can actually help to make things happen. Magical ideas include the notion that thought affects matter and that the trained imagination can alter the physical world, that all aspects of the Universe are interdependent and that we can discover connections and correspondences between everyday occurrences and cosmic, or Divine, energies. A miracle or a wish coming true can suggest something is going on that extends beyond the laws of nature, that something unseen has occurred; but just because we cannot see it or touch it, it doesn't mean it's not there. Magic exists, especially if you truly believe it does, but science is so far incapable of capturing its essence or the rationale behind it. Personally, I prefer to leave that task to the higher powers of the Universe.

To help your dreams come true and to use your inborn power to its full effect, you can employ boosters based on the special energies and qualities of your Sun sign. These 'boosters' are chosen to be in alignment with the purpose of a particular goal, and contain energies of their own which will enhance the strength of your spell, prayer, ritual or 'asking'. Specific magical energies can be invoked by carrying out a spell or ceremony using specific herbs or colours, or on a particular day of the week, according to either your Sun sign (to heighten the power of the asking), and/or that is in sympathy with that for which you are asking (I have included days of the week for other Sun signs and spell types).

Some materials and boosters you can use to increase the power, magic or energy in any area of your life include: candles, wish lists (written on an appropriate piece of paper written with a specially-chosen writing tool), symbols, affirmations, chants, incense, herbs and flowers, locations, colours, days of the week, elements, crystals and gemstones, animal symbols, charms, talismans, amulets, gods and goddesses, essential oils, planetary hours and your Solar totem animals. All are covered, some more briefly than others, for your very special Sun sign to radiate the energy to powerfully draw your wildest dreams towards you!

Overall, it pays to remember that the Universe (or whatever higher power/s or force/s you happen to believe in) creates *through* you that to which you give your attention. What you contemplate becomes the law of your being, and through your pure unwavering belief, is eventually brought through to manifestation on the material plane. What you think about is entirely up to you. But just be mindful that whatever you think about the most becomes your dominant thought, then your main point of attraction, and is ultimately magnified until it becomes your reality or your experience. So choose your thoughts with care. And to quote Ralph Waldo Emerson, "Be careful what you set your heart upon, for it will surely be yours." I carry a copy of this beautiful prophecy in my purse as its words resonate so strongly with me. In other words, be mindful about what you're wishing for, for you will most probably get it, whether it's good or bad - magic, after all, doesn't discriminate. Just make your dominant thoughts good ones, and you will attract everything you set your heart and intentions upon. Good luck!

ASTROLOGY & MAGIC

"Everyone practices magic, whether they realise it or not, for magic is the art of attracting particular influences, events and situations within human life. Magic is a natural phenomenon because the Universe is reflexive, responding to human thoughts, aspirations and desires ..."
David Fideler, *Jesus Christ, Sun of God*

Astrology is the most sublime of the occult * sciences, while at the same time it is one of the most practical for everyday application, for it divines the human soul itself. The cosmos, particularly the patterns that formed across it at the exact moment we were born, indicates the road along which our mental and spiritual endowments are likely to impel us, therefore enabling us to prepare in advance for life's battles, pitfalls, milestones, celebrations and of course to make the utmost of opportunities. Such is the magic of the human mind, that it can 'see' into the future and relive the past without having to be physically present in either, and when combined with astrological *knowing*, particularly the knowing that springs from understanding some of the dynamics of our natal chart, however basic, our inner - and outer - magic can be lifted to phenomenal heights.

In ancient times, not only was astrology the ardent study of the most learned and powerful minds, but among the masses of ordinary people its authority and guidance was accepted and followed without question. How this powerful knowledge was used was - and still is - up to the individual, but all who used it applied it to their perceived advantage.

As primitive humans observed the skies, no doubt they gradually realised that certain stars upon which their fate depended accompanied the seasons, or certain times of the year. They may also have reasoned that if governed their fate, they also governed their bodies, and it is therefore conceivable that the skies were associated with Divine influence. Certain celestial influences were believed to emanate from the thirty-six decans of the signs, and the mysterious but apparent effect that they exercised upon humans were thought to be due to a subtle ether shed by the heavenly stars and spheres on the Earth, that affected not only people, but also other animals, plants and minerals. For the ancient mind, linking magic with astrology may have also provided a much needed sense of predictability and patterns.

Early astrologers named and made associations with the imaginary divisions of the twelve signs and the twelve houses, and people born under a certain sign were said to inherit to an extent, its properties and nature. They also believed that the influence of the planets and stars corresponded with the medicinal properties of certain plants and minerals. They therefore asserted that the influence of a star or planetary position would affect the type of medicine or healing they would offer a subject to attain the most beneficial outcome. Throughout the writings of early philosophers and theorists, there is constant reference to this unmistakable mystic connection between the seven known planets and Earthly affairs and ailments. The seven metals were connected with the seven planets, to which the seven colours and the seven transformations were added. So the alchemist came to share the astrological doctrine that each planet ruled some mineral: The Sun ruled gold, the Moon silver, Mars iron, Venus copper **, Saturn lead, Jupiter tin, and Mercury quicksilver. Consequently, in alchemical symbolism the same sign came to represent the metal and its corresponding planet.

In subsequent years, astrology became closely related to alchemical knowledge and development, and the alchemist came to be regarded as an authority not only on the transmutation of metals, but also on astrology and magic. This goes some of the way to explaining how magic and divination, which had always been inseparably bound up with astrology, came to be associated with alchemy. In all the occult sciences, the supreme power was believed to be in the stars above, and from their mysterious emanations all the metals, crystals, minerals, plants and herbs derived their special properties over time. Further, as alchemy became ever more spiritual and concerned with more abstract and philosophical concepts, eventually it was considered that the transmutation of lead into gold was simply a metaphor for the transformation of base matter, in this case the human soul, into a much purer and higher state of wisdom and being.

The Sun and Moon were believed to have greater influence over the human body than all the other heavenly bodies, and to exert their influence in various ways whenever they entered a certain sign of the zodiac. And although the Moon was traditionally regarded as the most important factor of a horoscope, the Sun has come into its own in later centuries, with the result that almost everyone knows their Sun sign but only those who have delved deeper are aware of the sign their natal Moon falls in. For this reason, I have chosen to focus this book series on the twelve Sun signs, as this is what the majority of people are most familiar with.

The following pages contain methods, energies, materials and objects which may be used to increase the magic and power of your Sun sign's influence upon you. Precious stones, flowers, colours and so on, are regarded as having a potent effect upon good fortune by attuning your mind to receive harmonious vibrations from the astral forces that surround you.

Finally, a basic working knowledge of basic astronomy and astrology is an asset when working with luck, abundance, wealth and personal power. You can attract more of these things when you align yourself with the workings of the wider Universe, the movement of the Sun, stars, Moon and planets and become aware of the correlations between the outer cycles of the skies and the inner cycles within yourself. Also, for those who are knowledgeable about Moon phases, equinoxes and solstices, a world of lucky possibilities can also magically open up to you. You don't need to know about astrology's deepest complexities to understand how everything interrelates; just learning the basics will give you an edge - and hopefully the following lucky tips will provide you with at least a small glimpse into the insights gleaned from your Sun sign, which I am certain will endow upon you the potential for amazing results to manifest in your life - and maybe even a step up one further rung towards the heavens!

* The word 'occult' comes from the Latin *occultus*, which literally means 'knowledge of the hidden'.

** The alchemical sigil for copper represents the metal of Venus. It is assigned to this planet because it is a 'harmony' metal. Copper combines with other metals and, being soft and malleable, it is ideal for artisans to fashion into beautiful objects and adornments.

USING COLOURS, CRYSTALS, DEITIES, PLANTS, FOODS & MATERIAL SUBSTANCES FOR INCREASING POWER & MAGNETISING MAGIC

Alchemist, reformer and mystic Henry Cornelius Agrippa, born in 1486, in his principal work, *On Occult Philosophy*, expressed his belief in the doctrines of astrology and in the theory that the spirit of the world exists in the body of the world, just as the human spirit exists in the body of man. He contended that this spirit also abounds in the celestial bodies and descends in the rays of stars, so that the things influenced by their rays become conformable to them. By this spirit every occult property is conveyed into metals, stones, herbs and animals, through the Sun, Moon and planets, and even through the stars beyond and higher than the planets. A firm believer in the efficacy of charms, he stated that they may "be worn on the body bound to any part of it or hung around the neck, changing sickness into health or health into sickness." I believe the same effect could be applied to wishing and the thinking of positive thoughts, to mean, "Changing thoughts and dreams into manifest reality." He also recommended that these charms be worn in the form of finger rings (that have been created using the materials in agreement and harmony with your Sun Sign's magical energy).

Material substances are connected with abstract purposes by a complex but highly usable and accessible system of correspondences. Use these time-honoured connections in your own spells and wishes to magnetise your desires to you. The following pages will give you some materials, energies, forces and ideas you can summon the power of in order to enhance your magic and luck.

PLANETS

The Planetary influence of the day is important when 'asking' for something. If you are wishing for luck, for example, try working with your Sun sign's inherent energies combined with the perfect day of the week for it. So a Libran might try using his natural intellect and articulate expression, to ask for greater luck on a Thursday, which is Jupiter's Day and Jupiter is renowned for being a lucky planet, or better still, ask for luck on a Friday, which is Venus's Day, planetary ruler of Libra, at the time of day when Jupiter's influence is at its most powerful (information about planetary hours for each day of the week can be found on the Internet or in books on the subject, and can be complex and detailed. It is an art to memorise the correct times, days and energies for the correct spells. If you are determined enough to achieve your dream or goal however, you will be determined enough to put in the research to do it properly!) Here is a very simplified list of the days of the week and their meanings:

DAYS OF THE WEEK & THEIR POWERS

MONDAY ★ Moon
Cancer

The Divine feminine, changes, intuition, emotions, secrets, dealing with women, purity, goodness, perfection, unity, psychic ability, magic, spirituality, invoking a goddess's or angel's guidance, anything that fluctuates, contracts, increases or decreases.

TUESDAY ★ Mars
Aries & Scorpio

Enthusiasm, competition, passion, energy, courage, protection, victory, anything requiring assertiveness, standing up for yourself, or a 'fighting spirit', determination, vitality, sexuality, self-confidence, men's power, men's mysteries, drive, ambition, achievement, triumph, masculinity.

WEDNESDAY ★ Mercury
Gemini & Virgo

Education, travel, exams, study, communication, making connections, thinking, dealing with siblings, writing and speaking, knowledge, learning, adaptability, charm, youth, absorbing information.

THURSDAY ★ Jupiter
Sagittarius & Pisces

Increase and expansion of anything (remember to be careful what you wish for), luck, growth, influence, worldly power, accomplishment, fulfilment, gambling, philosophy, higher education, abundance, optimism.

FRIDAY ★ Venus
Taurus & Libra

Love, luxury, the arts, indulgence, beauty, marriage, money, prosperity, fertility, women's power, women's mysteries, grace, charm, appeal, hope, pleasure, decorating, self-worth, self-esteem, personal values, business partnerships, romance, creativity, sharing, bonding.

SATURDAY ★ Saturn
Capricorn & Aquarius

Long-term goals, career, institutions, establishments, security, investments, karma, reversal, structure, protection, solitude, privacy, determination, ending, blocking, renewing, transforming, anything to do with the public.

SUNDAY ★ Sun
Leo

All-purpose, success, wishes, generosity, happiness, optimism, spirit/essence, recognition, health, vitality, material wealth, invoking a god's aid or guidance, personal empowerment, spirituality, the Divine masculine.

YOUR NATAL MOON PHASE

Although this book is aimed at enhancing your life through the energy of your Sun sign, a bit of Lunar help can give your wishing a boost! As well as using the planetary days and hours system to add a bit of zest to your wish fulfilment, try combining your Sun sign's power periods with your natal Moon phase (your natal Moon phase can be calculated using a number of sources on the internet, or through an astrologer), or even studying which constellation the Moon is situated in at certain times, to increase the power of your spells and asking rituals. For example, you might like to 'ask' for a promotion at work during a New/Waxing Moon period, particularly if the Moon happens to fall under an auspicious sign for career advancement, such as Capricorn. Your natal Moon phase can also be used to similar effect, by researching when your Moon phase will coincide with a certain Lunar constellation position.

In most astrological interpretations the Sun is regarded as the most important, central feature of a natal chart. But to many the Moon is equally, if not more, important than the Sun sign. Many ancient cultures considered the Moon sign to be more significant. The Moon passes through the 12 signs about every 2.5 days, usually covering the whole zodiac in around 27.3 days. The Moon symbolises our inner world, the world of feeling, emotions, habitual responses, instincts, intuition, security and the subconscious. It describes our nurturing style and needs, our emotional response to life, our attitudes and likely reactions to others, our instinctive and habitual responses, the receptive feminine side of ourselves, our experience of our mother or mother figure, and our childhood experience. It represents the soul. In relationships it symbolises how we like to be nurtured and cared for, and the potential depth of our involvement on personal intimate levels.

For many centuries, people across the world have recognised that the Moon influences the affairs of all living things on planet Earth. The waxing Moon appears to have a drawing, increasing and enhancing effect, whereas the waning Moon has a decreasing, receding and withdrawing effect. All things that come into being are stamped with the qualities of the prevailing Moon stage. It seems that people born during certain Lunar phases tend to share specific attributes with other people born during this same phase. In turn, their attributes will be subtly different from those of individuals born during any of the other stages in the Moon cycle. Knowing exactly which phase of the Moon you were born under gives you all kinds of extraordinarily valuable insights into your character, emotions, behaviour and motivations in life. It can make you aware of your deepest underlying drives, the fundamental purpose that you are drawn towards in life and the contribution you can make to others and society during the course of your lifetime. This knowledge may enable you to intuit and make the most of your own personal cyclical pattern that you go through each month, and allow you to know when the most auspicious periods of time are for you and your affairs, nurture yourself and channel your energies in the most positive directions.

Because this Lunar pattern repeats itself every month, you will find that you can even pace yourself on a long-term basis. This will enable you to effectively target your efforts and goals on periods of time that you know will be potentially fortunate for you. You may in fact find that your birth phase corresponds with the days of the month when you have abundant energy, feel inspired and can generate new ideas with ease. During this period, you should work towards the fruition of your efforts, bring your dreams into light and reach for the stars!

The Lunar Phases Are:

★ New Moon
★ First/Waxing Crescent
★ First Quarter
★ Waxing Gibbous Moon
★ Full Moon
★ Waning Gibbous / Disseminating Moon
★ Last Quarter
★ Waning Crescent / Balsamic Moon
★ Back to the New Moon

SPELLS, MAGIC & WISHING WITH MOON PHASES

Though the Moon has eight astronomical phases, it is the three phases corresponding to maiden, mother and crone that are the most significant in spells, ritual, wish magic and psychic work. By tuning into the physical Moon we can understand and harness these distinct energy phases in our daily lives and magical worlds. The four primary Lunar phases are the New Moon, First Quarter, Full Moon and the Last Quarter. Depending on what sort of spell you wish to perform, your spell should take place during one of these cycles or time periods. Each phase of the Moon is good for some types of magic, but not so much for others.

NEW MOON, WAXING & FIRST QUARTER

In astronomical terms, the New Moon occurs when the Moon rises and sets at the same time as the Sun. Both bodies are found in the same position compared with the Earth. Therefore, a Solar eclipse can only ever occur at the New Moon, when the two luminaries are found, for a short time, in a perfect line relative to the Earth, with the Moon positioned between the Sun and the Earth. The New Moon's sunlit face is hidden from the Earth.

In astrological terms, the New Moon occurs at a time when the Sun and the Moon are found in the same degree of the zodiac and therefore occupy the same zodiac sign, forming a conjunction, or a 'fusing' of energies.

In astronomical terms, the First Quarter occurs seven days after the New Moon. Seen from the Earth, this phase makes the Moon like a crescent, forming the shape of a capital D.

In astrological terms, it occurs when the Sun and the Moon form a ninety-degree angle, or the square aspect, inside the zodiac, the Moon always preceding the Sun.

As the New Moon marks the beginning of a new cycle, it symbolises fresh starts. This is an exceptional time to work magic and make wishes for new beginnings, and for the conception and initiation of new projects. Use this Moon phase for improving health, the gradual increase of prosperity, attracting good luck, fertility magic, finding new love, friendship or romance, job hunting, making plans for the future and increasing your general spiritual or psychic awareness.

Overall, the Waxing Crescent and First Quarter Moon phases are appropriate for spells, rituals and workings that involve growth, healing and increase. This is a period of time lasting approximately two weeks, to draw things toward you and increase things, such as love, prosperity and new opportunities. During this period is the time to bless new projects, anything that requires energy to grow, such as gardens, business ventures, new homes, or educational pursuits. Personal growth and healing are accented, as is 'attraction magic' - drawing something to you such as love, abundance, health, success or a new path - and if done well, you can expect results by the next Full Moon. Magical workings for gain, increase or bringing things to you should be initiated when the Moon is waxing (or New, going from Dark to Full). A time for divination of all kinds, spells of spiritual intention, and for any creative project you wish to see birthed, with magical and fruitful results.

While making a wish within the first forty-eight hours after the New Moon is a powerful way of helping it come to fruition, the most potent time for making wishes is actually within the first eight hours of the exact time of its position. Write down your wish list within this first eight hours on a piece of appropriately coloured paper with a special writing tool, and be sure to capture the essence of your wish by wording it in a way that charges your emotions and simply feels 'right'. Make a maximum of ten wishes (less is perfectly fine too), as making too many wishes might disperse their energy too much to be effective. After writing down your list and releasing your wishes to the Universe in whichever form you feel happy with, keep your list and check on it in a few days', weeks' or months' time to assess whether anything has shifted in the direction of your listed dreams, desires or goals. I'll bet it has - or at the very least, something even better has arrived in its place!

Although the first forty-eight hours after the New Moon is the most potent time to make a special wish, you can begin Waxing Moon magic when you can see the crescent in the sky and continue until the day before the Full Moon. The closer to the Full Moon, the more intense the energies. In fact, a personally devised ritual using any special Lunar-associated materials over three days up to and including the Full Moon is excellent for something you require urgently or within a short timeframe.

In some cultures, people turn over silver coins or jewellery three times when the crescent Moon appears in the sky and make a wish. As the Moon grows, it is believed that prosperity and good fortune will grow too.

While the New Moon is not known as a time for 'banishing' or releasing things we no longer want in our lives, I feel that if we are to ask and wish for things, we need to make room to receive them. Making room means that the Universe can slot it right into our lives where we have cleared our paths for it. Clutter, unwanted things, unhappy relationships, possessions that no longer serve us, are all things we can banish. So, to help what you are asking for come into your life quicker, the New Moon is a particularly opportune time to throw a few things out so you can make way for the new and clear up some space for that which you are wishing for. What are you waiting for? Start creating a space for your wishes today!

FULL MOON

In astronomical terms, the Full Moon occurs 14 days after the New Moon, on the day when the Moon sets at the same time the Sun rises, or conversely. The two luminaries are effectively facing each other, with the Earth in between, the Sun shining its light onto the reflective Moon, giving it the fully lit up appearance of a giant, bright, perfectly round sphere. Indeed, its entire face is bathed in sunlight. A Lunar eclipse can only occur at the Full Moon, when the Sun, Moon and Earth are all in line, and the Earth hides the lit side of the Moon to us.

In astrological terms, a Full Moon occurs at the time when the Sun and Moon are 180 degrees apart inside the zodiac, and therefore positioned in opposite signs, forming an opposition aspect.

The highest energy occurs at the Full Moon, making this is a powerful time for all manner of magical workings. Use the Full Moon phase for any immediate need, a sudden boost of power or courage, psychic protection, a change of career or location, travel, healing acute health conditions, the consummation of love or a commitment, justice, ambition and promotion of all kinds. This phase lasts approximately 3 days - 24 hours before the exact Full Moon, the day of, and 24 hours after it, according to many sources - giving us 3 full days to perform our spells. However, we are not strictly limited to a three-day period; the power of this phase can actually be accessed for seven days - three days prior to, the night of, and the three days after the Full Moon. The Full Moon period is when the Moon is at her most powerful, being the most luminous and radiant part of the cycle. Known as the 'high tide' of psychic power, the Full Moon represents culmination, climax, fulfilment and abundance. The Full Moon governs all kinds of magic, including manifestation, banishing, and is particularly good for calling forth protection and heightening your intuitive abilities. The Full Moon contains magic that calls forth personal power, fertility, spiritual development, and psychic awareness. Cleansing of ritual tools, crystals, wish lists, Tarot decks, and the like can be done during this phase. Magic worked during the Full Moon often takes one complete cycle to come to fruition. Try also reaffirming your desires during the New Moon to give them an added nudge in the right direction.

LAST QUARTER OR WANING MOON

In astronomical terms, the Last Quarter, or Waning Moon, occurs twenty-one days after the New Moon. The time difference between the rising and setting of the two luminaries is reduced to what it was at the First Quarter. Viewed from the Earth, the Moon resembles a crescent whose lit up area is decreasing in size, forming the shape of a capital C.

In astrological terms, the Waning Moon occurs when the Sun and Moon are positioned at ninety degree angles of each other in the zodiac, forming the square aspect again. However, during this phase, the Sun is instead *ahead* of the Moon.

The Waning Moon represents the Lunar cycle from Full to Dark. Any spells and magic performed during this period is based purely around banishing and releasing. It could involve releasing things which no longer serve you (such as behaviours, material things, relationships and attitudes), banishing negative energies, and removing obstacles which are standing in the way of achieving your goals or dreams. The Waning Moon is the best time for cleansing, gently releasing, eliminating, expelling and completion. It is of great assistance when you are wanting to let go of something, or someone, gradually. The Dark of the Moon, the period when the Moon is no longer visible to the naked eye, until the New Moon, is the most useful time for divination of all kinds.

★ What is your natal Moon phase type? Can you think of ways you can combine it with the power of your Sun sign to effect change and bring about wonderful happenings? ★

HARNESSING YOUR PERSONAL MOON MAGIC ★ MOON IN LIBRA

When the Moon is in your sign of Libra, it is a great time for working magic around: Balance, harmony, love, relationships, marriage (an existing one or one wished for), beauty rituals, cooperation, courtesy and artistic pursuits. Suggested operations could be around rituals and spells to bring about sharing of the arts with others (music, painting, dance, writing, theatre, design), and an increase of love, friendship and relating skills in your life. Spells to help attract more social invitations, romance and leisure activities could be performed around this time to great effect. With the Moon in Libra, you can seek to make yourself more beautiful and attractive on the inside or out, to resolve conflicts through mediation, agreement, contracts or negotiation, to summon karmic or literal justice, and treat yourself and others more fairly. Justice, truth, getting along with others, tolerance, improvements in communication, partnerships of all kinds, and equality are all accentuated here.

THE MOON ★ WHAT IT REPRESENTS IN THE HUMAN PSYCHE & NATAL CHART

The Moon in the sky shines with the reflected light of the Sun. Although not a planet, the Moon is our nearest celestial neighbour and exerts a great influence upon us. The gravitational pull of the Moon affects our body fluids, which contribute to about 90 per cent of our biological make-up. It moves at approximately half a degree per hour and takes an average of 27.3 days to pass through all twelve zodiac signs, staying in each for around 2.5 days.

In astrology the Moon corresponds with the way in which we reflect and respond to what is going on around us. It has to do with our feelings, emotions and instincts and, in the same way the Moon influences the tides on planet Earth, it symbolises the ebb and flow of our emotional nature, our moods, fluctuations and changeability. The Moon is the archetype of the Mother, which is within us all, and represents the primary feminine principle in the natal chart. It is through the Moon that we express our parental instincts - caring, nurturing, protecting, sensitivity. The Moon has links with the past and the subconscious and it is from this almost primitive source that our natural instinctual forces flow.

The Moon is essentially a feminine principle and associates with the inner personality, receptivity, passivity and inward-oriented feelings. It can act as an inner guide to the deeper self, the unconscious self, figures half-shrouded in mystery, linking the hidden personal world of the subconscious to the clearer world of personal awareness.

The Moon is the innermost core of our being, private feelings, habitual reactions and subconscious habits. It is the caring, nurturing sustainer of life, the 'mother' of the zodiac. It tells us about how we seek security, our urge to nurture, our nurturing style, our responses and feelings and moods. The innermost core of our being, private feelings, subconscious habits. It is concerned with habits, mothering, habitual/instinctive responses and personality. It is our karma, our soul, our past.

The Moon represents our mother or mother figure, our feminine side, maternal instinct, our nurturing style and needs, our unconscious self, our emotional reactions, the subconscious, our feelings, instincts, intuition, receptivity, habits, what we need to feel secure, fluctuations, cycles, moods, and our childhood. Its position in the birth chart is very significant, because as well as revealing feminine qualities and the potential gentleness and tenderness of a being, the Moon also reveals important information about the experiences and expression of the five senses.

The Moon is essentially receptive and passive; it reflects the life experience rather than initiating it. Fluctuating and cyclical, the Moon is the planet (although technically a satellite) of the childhood experience, and instinctual reactions. It represents the mother (a child's experience and expectations of their mother), maternal instincts and the feminine principle, indicating how strongly these manifest in an individual, male or female.

As it represents what our childhood experience is likely to be, and childhood is essentially a time where our consciousness has not yet fully developed, our Moon sign traits seem to be more apparent in our younger years. We will usually show our Moon sign traits more so than our Sun sign traits during this developing period of infancy and early childhood, until we have the presence of mind to more consciously develop our ego and true core self (the Sun).

The symbol for the Moon ☽ is a representation of its crescent in its waxing phase from new to full, but it can also be seen as two half circles - these form a bowl shape, a receptacle, a feminine container that 'receives' and 'holds' anything put into it. The half circle, unlike the full circle of the Sun, is finite and incomplete, almost as if striving for wholeness.

The Moon represents our *soul*.

YOUR MOON SIGN

The Sun / Moon Polarity
Conscious & Unconscious, Night & Day, Yin & Yang

"Man does, woman is."
Edward Edinger

Your Moon Sign, representing your soul, and your Sun sign, representing your spirit, work together to form the foundation of your basic personality, expression and nature. If you know what your Moon sign is, look it up below and read how it works with your Libran Sun to blend your mind, soul and spirit.

♈ **With the Moon in ARIES, Sun in Libra,** you are likely to be ★ Conflicted between independence and needing others, diplomatic, sociable, gracefully bold, a rash judge, hospitable, entertaining, influential, convivial, convincing, cheeky, fun-loving, romantic, emotionally naïve, a peace-making crusader, gentle yet impulsive, intriguing, able to make sound judgements, gregarious, the ability to win others over, assertive, temperamental, insensitive, ambitious, considered, polite, charming, avidly intellectual, persuasive, aesthetic, attractive, athletically elegant, respectful of others' opinions, pioneering, original, lively, witty, bright, breezy, an intelligent individualist, and one who has moral integrity.

Sun/Moon Harmony Rating ★ 8 out of 10

♉ **With the Moon in TAURUS, Sun in Libra,** you are likely to be ★ Calm, level-headed, pragmatically intellectual, easy going, possessive, hedonistic, lacking in depth, artistic, creative, aesthetically aware, stylish, affectionate, nurturing, emotionally generous, cooperative, lacking in depth, loving, gullible, considerate, thoughtful, gentle, infinitely patient, slow and steady-paced, tasteful, loving of music and art, indulgent, sociable, emotionally placid, pleasant, faithful, friendly, manipulative, philanthropic, thoughtful, comfort- and pleasure-seeking, impartial, effortlessly charming, a connoisseur, realistic, sensible, prudish, and dedicated to grounding your inspiration and idealism.

Sun/Moon Harmony Rating ★ 8.5 out of 10

♊ **With the Moon in GEMINI, Sun in Libra,** you are likely to be ★ Intellectual, a free spirit and social butterfly, friendly, bright, breezy, conciliatory, emotionally versatile, quick-witted, perceptive, clever, childlike, inspiring, inconsistent, unreliable, stimulating, youthful, questioning, carefree, flirtatious, versatile, articulate, casual, sociable, funny, detached, curious, impulsive, restless, easily bored, flighty, uncommitted, communicative, socially aware, emotionally naïve, entertaining, good with words and ideas, socially gifted, reasonable, clear-minded, emotionally immature, lazy, a wonderful friend, popular, easily swept away, open, likeable, idealistic, squandering of your natural talents, reluctant to face the darker aspects of life, shallow, cunning, a trickster, and ruled almost exclusively by your intellect.

Sun/Moon Harmony Rating ★ *7.5 out of 10* **

♋ **With the Moon in CANCER, Sun in Libra,** you are likely to be ★ Harmonious, tactful, sensitive, diplomatic, graceful, loving, poised, nurturing, emotional, able to blend emotions with intellect, intuitive, aesthetic, tasteful, elegant, affectionate, compassionate, quietly charming, caring, tender, focused on domestic harmony, refined, exquisitely composed, intimate, devoted, a peacemaker, attached, dependent, sharing, sympathetic, understanding, artistically imaginative, peaceful, finicky, ethereal, vulnerable, intelligently kind, helpful, companionable, manipulative, subjective, clingy, socially timid but sociable, courteous, understatedly stylish, affable, pleasant, over-romanticising, easily unbalanced, supportive of others, and concerned for others.

Sun/Moon Harmony Rating ★ *8 out of 10*

♌ **With the Moon in LEO, Sun in Libra,** you are likely to be ★ Popular, gracious, vacillating, chivalrous, vain, relationship-seeking, likable, companionable, artistically inspired, desiring to uplift and encourage others, diplomatic, glamorous, elegant, pleasure-seeking, commanding, leisurely, individualistic but sociable, optimistic, indecisive, dependent on others for your wellbeing and self-confidence, gracefully dramatic, artistic, generous, subtly passionate, radiant, enthusiastic, romantic, open, easily flattered, charismatic, charming, self-indulgent, hedonistic, inclined to get carried away by romance and idealism, eager for praise, friendly, expressive, reliant on others' admiration, self-centred, intelligently creative, addicted to love, warm, engaging, playful, tasteful, refined, luxury-loving, demonstrative, creatively imaginative, vivacious, big-hearted, aesthetically aware, civilised, a visionary, trusting, ardent, affectionate, a gentle wit, noble, and appealing to others.

Sun/Moon Harmony Rating ★ 8 out of 10

♍ **With the Moon in VIRGO, Sun in Libra,** you are likely to be ★ Intelligent, judgemental, courteous, devoted to helping others, detached, focused on justice and fairness, aloof, calm and collected, refined, loving of purity and simplicity, finicky, eminently civilised, self-critical, clever, indecisive yet discerning, cooperative, discriminating, independent, understatedly witty, rational, reasonable, trying to achieve emotional balance, civilised, sensual, fussy, tasteful, prudish, scathing of crudeness, methodical, nit picking, studious, gentle, kind, helpful, mentally alert, unassuming, efficient but often procrastinating, caring, understated, quality-seeking, coolly reserved, socially conventional, polite, objectively rational, cool-headed, altruistic, genuinely kind, bright, and devoted to both ideas and ideals.

Sun/Moon Harmony Rating ★ 6 out of 10

♎ **With the Moon in LIBRA, Sun in Libra,** you are likely to be ★ Sociable, idealistic, co-dependent, elegant, indecisive, charming, flirtatious, refined, well-balanced, easy going, moderate, easy going, sharing, loving, manipulative, affectionate, popular, inspired, graceful, approachable, accessible, civilised, sharing, gracious, cooperative, hospitable, hedonistic, romantic, observant, loving of people, delightful, persuasive, artistically sensitive, naïve, and conflicted between independence and needing others.

Sun/Moon Harmony Rating ★ 8 out of 10

♏ **With the Moon in SCORPIO, Sun in Libra,** you are likely to be ★ Sociable, intense, intriguing, self-possessed, astutely minded, artistically charged, lustful, sensitive, promiscuous, highly charged, magnetic, possessive of others, moody, emotionally intelligent, intuitive, easily unbalanced, keenly insightful, investigative, strongly focused on justice, ethereally mysterious, socially regenerative, in possession of strong desires, prone to temptation, conflicted between extreme and moderate behaviours, strong-willed, self-judging, appealing, socially passionate, broody, suspicious, paranoid, resourceful, resilient, secretive, manipulative, passionate yet dispassionate, emotionally influential and charismatic, courageous, incisive, a good observer, and acutely perceptive.

Sun/Moon Harmony Rating ★ 7 out of 10

♐ **With the Moon in SAGITTARIUS, Sun in Libra,** you are likely to be ★ Persuasive, eager to please others, hopeful, expressive, loving of life, joyful, generous, adventurous, well-received, calm yet restless, ardent but flighty, enthusiastic, independent, open, idealistic, an intellectual philosophiser, objective, spirited, a believer, romantic, impatient with restrictions of daily life, wise, indecisive, socially charged, intellectual, interested, engaged, one who brings out the best in others, engaging, sociable, inquisitive, easy going, inspiring, a traveller, an avid student of life, clever, witty, charming, warm, distant from your feelings, emotionally reckless, a free spirit, far-sighted, positive, knowledgeable, good-humoured, self-promoting, emotionally naïve, optimistic, inspiring, aspiring, gregarious, socially caring, direct but courteous, broad-minded, expansive, trusting, verbose, emotionally philosophical, and guided by reason rather than emotion.

Sun/Moon Harmony Rating ★ *8.5 out of 10*

♑ **With the Moon in CAPRICORN, Sun in Libra,** you are likely to be ★ An introverted people-liker, purposeful, dependable, persuasive, Earthy yet ethereal, fair, rational, courteous, sophisticated, ambitious, graceful, sensual, resourceful, committed, aloof, distant from your feelings, dutiful, self-interested yet cooperative, tidy, pragmatic, tasteful, orderly, tactful, well-mannered, reserved, cool, gentle, wise, kind-hearted, strategic, skilful at managing people, sensitive to social nuances, responsible, dedicated to those you love, shrewd, efficient and effortless, opportunistic, manipulative, controlling, reliable, socially serious, sensible, materialistic, hedonistic, reliant on the physical senses for pleasure, understanding of practical applications and wisdom, personally honourable, adhering to morals, torn between solitude and sociability, uptight, self-contained, aware of human relationships, and sardonically humorous.

Sun/Moon Harmony Rating ★ *7 out of 10*

♒ **With the Moon in AQUARIUS, Sun in Libra,** you are likely to be ★ Frank, easy going, original, tolerant, friendly, independent yet dependent, torn between freedom and needing others, sociable, idealistic, emotionally detached, gracefully eccentric, one with unconventional tastes, glamorously aloof, cool, mysterious, paradoxical, intriguing, imaginative, thoughtful, humane, sympathetic, honest, unassuming, forward-moving, inventive, impersonal in relationships, objective, clear-headed, observant, aware of the human condition, progressive, scientifically and intellectually oriented, living an unusual lifestyle in some way, well-meaning, open to the unusual, emotionally naïve, trusting, rational, outgoing, communicative, gracefully anarchistic, truth-seeking, receptive, artistically refined, principled, just, fair, romanticising of others, socially conscious, open to new ideas, approachable, beauty-focused, over-identifying with causes and people, torn between freedom and commitment in relationships, a people-lover, unorthodox, impractical, scatterbrained, loyal, a humanitarian, committed to your ideals, focused on both Universal and the personal realms of experience, lazy, naïve, ineffectual, a dreamer, blind to your dependence on others, and potentially a genius.

Sun/Moon Harmony Rating ★ 8 out of 10 **

♓ **With the Moon in PISCES, Sun in Libra,** you are likely to be ★ Intuitive, socially graceful, quietly charming, highly imaginative, able to blend rationality and mysticism, confused, ethereal, gullible, impractical, spiritual, deeply idealistic, co-dependent, a chaser of spiritual rainbows, idolising of others, relationship-oriented, cooperative, helpful, adaptable, kind-hearted, good-natured, intriguing, mysterious, too trusting, friendly, accessible, approachable, emotional, apt to go into flights of fancy, sentimental, accepting, forgiving, understanding, vulnerable, a thinker and a poet, insightful, generous, idle, lazy, reflective, manipulative, receptive, creative, reverent, empathetic, compassionate, a humanitarian, prone to drifting and wasting time in daydreams, impressionable, idealistic but easily swayed, evasive, sensitive, psychic, perceptive, emotionally intelligent, ruled by your feelings, able to mix and work with all types of people, aware of the needs of others, artistic, wistful, inconstant, changeable, a dreamy romantic, loving, moody, involved, wishy-washy, helpful, and lacking in conviction.

Sun/Moon Harmony Rating ★ 8 out of 10

** If your Moon is in Gemini or Aquarius, your Sun and Moon will form what is known in astrology as a trine aspect. This aspect is the easiest, most flowing and harmonious astrological aspect, ensuring that your Sun and Moon, or spirit and soul, are well integrated. With both luminaries in Air signs, this gives them the best possible degree of complementary energy - a blending of the elements suggests a balanced expression of personality. One drawback of the trine aspect lies in the fact that its easy flow can be *too* harmonious; if our path is too smooth and difficulties don't arise to challenge us from time to time, we can often become lazy and complacent, stunting our growth and spiritual evolution. As Air signs, you share the art of sociability, are highly idealistic, affable, romantic, possess a good intellect, have a love of truth and beauty, are reasonable, broad-minded, independent but devoted to your ideals, have an artistic sensitivity, are tolerant, understanding, civilised and dignified, and have avant-garde tastes, but may be detached, cool, head over heart-oriented, and restless.

YOUR BODY & HEALTH

> "A physician without a knowledge of astrology has no right to call himself a physician."
> **Hippocrates (born c. 460 BC)**

Hippocrates, the fifth century BC Greek physician and 'father of medicine' and supposed author of the Hippocratic Oath, maintained that no one should be allowed to practise medicine who had not first studied astrology. Another Greek physician, Claudius Galen, brought together a huge range of knowledge and ideas in the second century AD which dominated medical practice until the 17th century. Among his teachings was a diagnostic technique which assumed that illnesses and their treatments were affected by and governed by the phases of the Moon. For centuries, astrology was a compulsory component of medical training (and still is in some natural medicine degrees), albeit only one aspect of diagnosis and treatment.

Medical or health astrology concerns particular ways of determining and interpreting an individual's horoscope with particular reference to health issues - diagnosis of current dis-eases, identification of areas of bodily weaknesses, and the prescription of natural cures and remedies. In ancient times, and still even today, the movement of the stars and planets was believed to affect bodily functions, and to cause ailments, or cure them.

During the Middle Ages, many drawings of the 'zodiac man' were made, which showed which signs of the zodiac were related to each part of the body, providing information as to the best times of the year to undertake cures for ailments affecting the corresponding body parts.

Health astrology persists today in many forms and among astrologers themselves, from whom clients seek counsel on health-related issues, and while it certainly cannot be used diagnose a condition or dis-ease, one's Sun sign, along with other factors of the natal chart, can definitely indicate potential problem areas of weakness or possible troubles. This branch of astrology has been found to be surprisingly accurate in most cases. While mostly accurate, none of the following information should ever be used as a substitute for professional medical advice should you be personally concerned about any of the conditions or afflictions listed for your Sun sign.

LIBRAN HEALTH

Libra is associated with the Kidneys, Skin, Glands, Fallopian Tubes, Urethra, Loins, Vasomotor System, Lumbar Region (Lower Back), Lumbar Vertebrae, Adrenals (with Aries), Acid/Alkaline, Sugar and Temperature Balance, Ears, Blood Vessels, Lower Back and the walls of the blood cells. It particularly governs the kidneys, lumbar regions and skin, and its subjects are liable to suffer from disorders affecting these parts, such as stones, lumbago, nephritis, diabetes, eczema and other eruptive skin conditions, as well as urinary troubles and diabetic conditions. Liquid processes are also associated with Libra.

Libra represents the energy of balance. Libra's nature is hot, moist and balancing. Principal rulerships include all endocrine glands, ureters, bladder, physical balance and Eustachian tube *, regulation of acid/alkaline balance in the body, systems of homeostasis, metabolism/thyroid balance, hormones and ovaries. As a result of any imbalance, you may experience bladder or urinary infections, skin troubles, fluid retention, thyroid/metabolic problems, hormone issues, lower back pain and high blood pressure caused by kidney conditions. Chronic back ache, kidney stones and urological issues may feature in your life. Ensure you drink plenty of purified water and herbal teas to maintain and keep your sensitive equilibrium in balance, to help clear up any skin disorders, and to keep your kidneys cleansed and healthy. You fare well on an alkaline-style diet with an abundance of fresh fruits, vegetables and juices, and adequate water. Seafood's and iodine-rich foods are important to support your metabolic and thyroid functions.

As an Air sign, your nerves are also prone to overstrain, and you should avoid over-worry, depression and stress. Living or working alone for long periods can be detrimental to Libran health, which may manifest as the typical illnesses attributed to your sign: ailments to do with the back, kidneys, skin, and anything that affects the body's equilibrium.

Although Libran people usually enjoy fairly good health, you are not as robust as you seem. Your constitution is very delicate and easily upset by minor ailments and psychological conflicts. The basic health rule for Librans is moderation in all things. You have a strong distaste for any discordant conditions and too much psychological conflict. You have a natural revulsion for excessive noise, loud people, disharmonious surroundings, vulgarity, coarseness - and just about every other antisocial vibration.

You should also guard against any Venus-ruled conditions or afflictions, such as those affecting the following parts of the body or bodily systems, which Venus rules (and some of which it shares with Libra): Thymus and Thyroid Glands, Venous Circulation, Saliva Ducts, Hormones, Kidneys, Sugar Balance, Hair Shafts and Production, Skin, Neck and the Throat, the Inner Ear, Balance and the Centre of Gravity. Venus is also associated with the Chin, Complexion, Cheeks, Viral Infections, and complaints caused by excesses or pleasures.

Whatever ails you, you will recover most quickly from illness if in pleasant, calm surroundings. Keeping yourself in excellent health overall, with a special awareness of Libra's vulnerable points, is key to achieving all you set out to do, and getting the most out of your life!

* The Eustachian tube is a narrow passage leading from the pharynx to the cavity of the middle ear, permitting the equalisation of pressure on each side of the eardrum.

THE CELL SALTS ★ ASTROLOGICAL TONICS

Homeopathy and astrology have colluded to provide a wonderful list of astrological tonics, one particularly suited to each of the twelve signs. These are called 'homeopathic cell salts', 'tissue salts' or 'biochemic cell salts', and are available in most health food stores, are inexpensive and easy to take. They are considered to be gentle, effective and safe, even for children, people in fragile health states, and the elderly. Although the full picture, drawn from a full natal horoscope, gives a fuller, more accurate idea of an individual's unique constitution, even simply working with one's date of birth can be enough for the medical astrologer to suggest the use of a cell salt based upon the correlation with an individual's Sun sign. As well as the cell salts having a significant effect upon physical ailments, they can also profoundly influence the subtle energy bodies, including the mental, emotional, etheric and spiritual. Although the most common use of these salts is based upon each salt's correspondence with a Sun sign, use of the cell salt related to one's Moon sign can assist with addressing deeper underlying emotional issues, such as anxiety, depression, panic and fear. Use of the cell salt relating to your Moon sign will therefore help to restore your sense of safety, balance, security and emotional resilience. In the first seven years of life, when the Moon is the most influential sphere in our lives, Lunar cell salts are the most appropriate choice as a remedy or tonic.

For specific health problems, take both the salt of your Sun or Moon sign, *and* the salt that pertains to the specific condition. The same principle applies to the Ascendant sign, as the First House represents one's physical health, and especially if the Sun or Moon is a rising planet, which means rulership of the whole chart. For the purposes of this book, however, the cell salt that correlates with your Sun sign only is outlined.

TISSUE SALT FOR LIBRA ★ NAT PHOS.

Natrium Phosphate, or Nat Phos. (Sodium phosphate) is the cell salt for Libra. Found in blood, muscles, nerve and brain cells, and intracellular fluid, it converts lactic acid into its by-products. It regulates the body's acid/alkaline balance, preventing an excess of either, especially in the bloodstream, and catalyses lactic acid and fat emulsion. Being a sign whose balance and equilibrium is easily upset, Librans need this cell salt to harmonise the balance between acids and alkalis. This is the biochemic acid stabiliser, so is useful in the prevention or treatment of such conditions as gout, digestive upsets, heartburn, stomach acidity, kidney stones and ulcers; in fact, all complaints arising from over-acidity respond well to this salt. If you detect an overly active pH in either your saliva or your urine, this is a prime indicator of dis-ease. Nat Phos., along with plentiful fresh fruit and vegetables, can help to correct this. It is also a remedy of choice for intestinal worms and other parasites. Psychologically, Nat Phos. is helpful in restoring emotional balance, especially after mental exertion or exposure to traumatic, tense or stressful situations or environments.

AIR SIGN LIBRA & THE SANGUINE HUMOUR

Greek physician Hippocrates (460 - 370 BC) theorised that certain human behaviours were caused by body fluids, called 'humours'. Later, Galen of Pergamon (AD 131 - 200), a Greek physician, developed the first typology of temperaments to encompass many facets of the human psyche and physiology. These also related to the classical elements of Fire, Earth, Air and Water - as choleric, melancholic, sanguine and phlegmatic respectively. According to the Greeks who developed the temperament theory (the word stems from the Latin word *temperamentum*, meaning mixture), temperament is the 'mixture' of qualities that combine to form elements in physics and humours in medicine. The Greeks sought equilibrium in the four qualities of hot, cold, wet (moist), and dry, the elements of Earth, Air, Fire and Water, and the four humours of choler or yellow bile, melancholer or black bile, blood and phlegm. If balance was achieved, the person was said to be well- or even-tempered, and the importance of determining the temperament allowed for imbalances to be treated.

In ancient times, each of the four types of humours corresponded to a different personality type, which were associated with a domination of various biological functions. It was suggested that the temperaments came to clearest manifestation in childhood, between around the ages of six and fourteen of age, after which they become subordinate, but still influential, factors in our personality. It is important to note that your temperament is not your personality. However, your personality can incorporate parts of the temperament in its expression. Personality is shaped by both external and internal factors, whereas the temperament is innate, an inborn, inherent part of each individual.

The Air element corresponds with the humour sanguine, which is characterised by quick, impulsive and relatively short-lived reactions. Sanguine types are analogous with Air, which is the main element in spring, the season with which this temperament has an affinity. Sanguine characters are ruled by Venus and Jupiter, hence the labels Venusian and Jupiterian Sanguines.

Sanguine types are driven by the need for attention and acceptance, social contact, relating, relationships, and trying to impress others. A sanguine disposition represents positivity, optimism, extroversion, expressiveness, talkativeness, and light-heartedness. You are generally responsive, carefree, easy going and lively.

Overall, a sanguine disposition represents sociability and openness. Its taste is bitter, its nature acidic, its indication blood. The sanguine humour is associated with the *gas* ^ body, and with hot and moist conditions.

---

^ A couple of thousand years ago, the Mesopotamians, Chinese and Egyptians, and more recently the Arabs, practised a medicine called 'of three bodies'. According to the doctors of the ancient world (who often practised as astrologers as well), a human being had three bodies: the physical body, the ethereal (or vital) body and the astral body, imparting a holistic approach to health. In modern medicine, usually only the physical body is focused upon fully. According to tradition, this physical body comprises three principles or states corresponding to three primordial elements: *solid* (Earth), *liquid* (Water) and *gas* (Air). This is the material body, the physical outer cover of muscles, nerves and organs held together by the skeleton. The Fire element corresponds with the *astral* body, which sits outside the physical body in one's auric field.

MONEY ATTRIBUTES

Colour for Increased Earning Power ★ Green

The following plants can be used by all zodiac signs to assist in attracting money ★ Ginger, Allspice, Clover, Orange, Marjoram, Cinnamon, Sassafras, Woodruff, Bergamot, Tonka Beans, Heliotrope, Alfalfa, Coltsfoot, Thyme, Mace, Irish Moss, Clove, Almond, Corn, Honeysuckle, Sesame, Nutmeg, Vetiver, Poppy, Jasmine, Dill and Elder Flower. To attract luck and success, try using any of the above, combined with any of the following: Alfalfa Seeds, Basil, Mustard Seeds, Vervain Leaves, Poppy Seeds, Rosemary, Lemon, Anise and Holly.

Striving for financial gain and abundance with a healthy inner moral compass is, in my view, one of the most noble goals we can set for ourselves. When we have more money, we are better placed to help ourselves and of course others; after all, as Abraham Maslow's Hierarchy of Needs model (1943) attests, once our primary and base survival needs have been satisfied, we can then advance higher towards loftier achievements, such as self-confidence, creativity and self-actualisation. Prosperity allows us to turn our attention to these more transcendental matters - to reach for lives not just of material comfort and luxuries, but of meaning, generosity, balance, harmony, fulfilment and joy. Our Sun sign can offer clues as to how we go about acquiring, earning, saving, maintaining, and allowing the overall flow of giving and receiving money. What's *your* money style?

Libran New Age author Stuart Wilde once said, "The key to success is to raise your own energy; when you do, people will naturally be attracted to you. And when they show up, bill 'em!" This quip reveals much about the Scales' financial nature, in that being of the Air element, you are naturally quite gifted when it comes to charming money right out of people's wallets.

You are interested in making money in partnership with another person, but often need to seek the advice of a professional financial advisor to diversify your finances. You may be indecisive and lazy when it comes to handling money, preferring to allow others to make things happen for you. Money seems to fall into your lap without too much effort on your part because of this. You may also be meticulous about financial planning, but find yourself in debt on account of the love of a good lifestyle. Fortunately, you always seem to earn enough to pay off any debt. Libran investments are carefully researched and designed to achieve long-term security, but only when you can be bothered. Always generous and willing to spend on luxury and quality, Libra loves to window shop and can never resist a bargain.

Vague and indecisive as you are, you know one thing for sure: you like to look your best, wear beautiful clothes and have lovely things around you. Because of this, you need a steady stream of money. Librans seem to have no trouble finding a partner to support their extravagant tastes and lifestyles too, so may find themselves in the fortunate position of not having to necessarily work more or earn more money than they absolutely have to.

If you are not careful, your outgoings often exceed your income, mainly because you adore giving presents and buying luxuries. Although you may appear quite open, you seldom reveal the whole truth of your financial situation. And despite your easy going approach to personal money, you have excellent business acumen.

Usually your money prospects are good and wealth, or at least prosperity, tends to flow to Venus subjects, whether through their careers, investments in luxuries, legacy or a fortunate marriage.

COLOURS

Chromatomancy, or divination by colour, is a form of energy therapy that has been used for thousands of years by many different cultures. It works on the principle that we make both instinctive and rational choices or preferences based on circumstances which are already present in ourselves; colour also has an effect on the energy in an environment, and we in turn respond consciously or subconsciously to our surroundings. If we look at the causes, and try to understand the reasons, as to why we are so receptive to one particular colour over another, we will see that there is a subtle link between certain hues and our emotional and instinctive individual reactions. The colour which we give to things results from a combination of three elements:

1. The light or the vibration of a body;

2. The context in which it is found and the interaction between its own light and that of its environment;

3. The sensitivity of the eye's retina which sees the body in question. Because of this, a colour can vary, depending on the individual's perceptions, namely, his sensitivity, his mood, and his view of reality. For a long time, people have understood that their vision of reality depends a lot on their moods, feelings and emotions.

Chromatotherapy, or colour healing, stems from this body of evidence, and its main application is the use of colours for healing purposes. Colours are generally associated with characteristics, feelings, stones, metals, plants and flowers, planets and even the zodiac signs. In varying cultures, they play a significant role in ceremonies and regalia.

We vibrate to the frequency of colour, shown through its continual movement and change in our aura ^. One of the most beautiful examples of colour is the rainbow. This architect of colour is caused by the refraction and internal reflection of light in raindrops. Colour can be perceived as either a pigment, or as illumination. The colour spectrum can be divided into eight main colours: red, orange, yellow, green, turquoise, blue, violet and magenta. Each colour has a wavelength and frequency that carry different therapeutic qualities which have indirect effects upon our health and bodily systems, and because of this, coupled with the fact that we as living energy centres emanate colour, colour can be a great medium in healing, calming, energising, increasing and attracting.

Aristotle, in the fourth century BCE, considered blue and yellow to be the true primary colours and related them to life's polarities: Sun and Moon, male and female, stimulation and sedation, in and out, expansion and contraction. He also associated colours with the four elements of Fire, Earth, Air and Water. Hippocrates, the father of medicine, used colour extensively in medicinal healing and recognised that the therapeutic effects of a white violet differed from those of a purple one. In the fifteenth century, Paracelsus placed particular importance on the role of colour in healing.

Each Sun sign and planetary body has a specific colour or colours which when used in combination with wishing rituals, can enhance their power immensely. Coloured candles can be used to good effect, as the fire energy of the flame/s increases the power of any wish, and flames are also a useful aid to meditating on, focusing upon or clarifying what you want. Coloured candles help to focus the energy for whatever purpose the colour is in sympathy with (e.g. green for money, pink for romance, orange for joy, etc.)

With all this in mind, wearing or using your Sun sign or ruling planet's magical colour/s on a regular basis will undoubtedly bring great benefits.

^ The aura is defined as an energy field, which interpenetrates with, and radiates beyond, the physical body. Clairvoyantly seen, the aura is full of light, colour and shade. The trained healer or seer sees or senses indications within the aura as to the spiritual, physical and emotional state of the individual. Much of the auric colour and energy emanates from the chakras.

YOUR LUCKY COLOURS

For Libra ★ Blue, Violet, Dark Crimson, Amber, Lemon Yellow, Light Blue, Green, Pink, All Pastel Shades, particularly Rose, Aqua and Light Green (balance with Indigo Blue)

For Venus ★ Blue, Pink, Yellow, Green

Ruled by Venus, you are naturally drawn to pink and blue. Because you are more ambitious and dynamic than your fellow Venusian-ruled Taurus, you tend to favour stronger sapphire blue.

Each of the eight colours of the rainbow spectrum also has a complementary colour to which it is matched. Red is complementary to turquoise, orange to blue, yellow to violet, and green to magenta. If these colour pairs enhance each other's most spellbinding qualities and energies, perhaps you could try wearing your Sun sign's lucky colour with its matching complementary colour in order to produce extra magical results! Your lucky Libran colours are pink, and blue - which complements orange. Now you know your colours, you can dress for success!

FEATURE COLOURS ★ PINK & BLUE

★ PINK ★

Planetary Association ★ Venus

Healing Qualities ★ Love, Thankfulness, Tenderness, Joy, Compassion, Romance, Happiness

Keywords ★ Partnerships, Beauty, Friendship, Venus, Friday, Femininity, Soft

Pink is a colour of Venus and is therefore known as the colour of love, affection, femininity, and soft joy. To the eye, pink is a very gentle, subtle colour which imbues one with serenity, balance, peace and tranquillity. The pink palette includes salmon, 'hot' pink *, coral, shell and rose pink, as well as cyclamen, cerise, fuchsia and magenta. Rose pink symbolises romantic love and encourages sympathetic feelings between people generally. It is closely aligned with how you relate to others. This love is not just the love you have for others, but also how you love yourself, with total acceptance and without egotism. It is considered a gentle colour: deeper shades represent gratitude and appreciation, while lighter shades signify admiration and sympathy. Pink is a romantic and tender colour, that softens the most hardened of hearts and relieves tension. Spaces with pink hues have been found to have a tranquillising effect and reduce the incidence of aggression in potentially volatile or hostile environments, such as prisons. Pink crystals are important in crystal healing, primarily because they bring balance to the Heart chakra, which in turn is your centre of balance. Working with pink gems can also help you deal with the trauma of a relationship breakdown and will help to heal the heart.

Pink contains both the Fire and Air elements and is a very useful colour to use in crystal therapy when treating conditions such as anger, anxiety, frustration or fear. Further, it is believed to attract love when used in spells, rituals, and other magical workings: pink candles, ribbons, gemstones and charms, for example, can elicit love when combined with belief and intention. In Feng Shui, pink is the colour of the south-west and represents marriage and partnership, so is a good colour choice for marital bedroom walls, bedding or decorative accessories; and a pink-painted house is believed to signify marital bliss and may enhance your partnership. It serves two, polar purposes: it represents child-like innocence, but it also signifies flirtation and the potential to lose one's purity. The Taj Mahal in India, the greatest monument to love in the world, exudes a pink aura which confirms this state of being. The gender politics of pink have a convoluted history: initially pink, not powder blue, was considered the traditional colour for baby boys, as it was a toned-down version of the fiercer red. However, in Nazi Germany, pink triangle patches were used to identify and imprison gay men and for decades after WWII, homosexuality remained illegal worldwide. Pink came to be not considered a 'manly' colour. Today, however, the pink triangle has been reclaimed as a positive symbol of the gay community and as such, it represents a culture of inclusiveness, not persecution. If you want to feel supported by Universal love you should wear more of this shade, but if you are feeling overwhelmed or 'fenced in', you should avoid it. Pink is the colour most likely to reduce stress or to create the 'rosy glow' we enjoy in positive and nurturing environments. It can be used in healing to promote fidelity, friendships, romance, subtlety, and tranquillity. Pink is an overall positive, calming colour which helps to transform negativity, hostility or resentment, into a more vibrant, positive energy at a deep level.

* A trend-setting pink, which was an attention-grabbing magenta, was named 'shocking pink' in the thirties, 'hot pink' in the fifties, and 'kinky pink' in the sixties, and was a fashion leader and bold statement in each of these eras.

The colour pink came into vogue through its proliferated use in the cosmetics industry during the sixties - a most defining and memorable decade - when no stylish woman would leave the house without her trusty pink lipstick. At other times, it took back position in the make-up chest and was dismissed as vulgar, sensational, ostentatious and showy.

★ BLUE ★

Planetary Associations ★ The Sun *, Venus

Blue is said to be the true colour of the Sun

Complementary Colour ★ Orange

Healing Qualities ★ Soothing, Clarity, Calming, Protective, Mental Control, Sedative, Communication, Productivity, Purifying

Keywords ★ Healing, Tranquillity, Thoughtfulness, Peace, Calmness, Water, Venus, The Sky, Truth, Inspiration, Higher Wisdom, Sincerity, Knowledge, Integrity

The colour of Jupiter and the element of Water, blue can be used for healing, clarity, improving perception, protection, sincerity, study and success. Blue has long been associated with healing, calming the mind and enhancing communication. It is the first colour we recognise when we see coloured objects - our eyes contain more receptive cells for blue than for any other colour. Indeed, the largest expanses we see are this hue - the sea and the sky.

Blue is cooling, calming and inspires mental clarity and inner peace. It gives us a sense of security and has been shown to lower blood pressure by quietening the autonomic nervous system. The colour blue symbolises inspiration, devotion, peace and tranquillity, and is a sedating and excellent healing colour. Blue creates a sense of space, so any room or area painted in this colour will appear larger or longer. Because of its calming vibes, it is a soothing and useful colour with which to treat headaches, tension, stress and insomnia. Blue is also one of the easiest colours to wear, it looks smart and sophisticated and there is some shade that will flatter everyone. It has the added value of encouraging focused mental effort and concentration. Lacking in intensity and not making an outstanding impression, it can be nonetheless intriguing and combined with other colours can take on a more dramatic effect.

Many shades of blue take their names from natural phenomena and life forms, for example: sky, ice, teal, peacock, duck-egg, gentian, indigo, cornflower, sapphire and aquamarine. It also has a long history of connections with the Divine - both spiritual and religious. However, blue is sometimes regarded as a gloomy or sad colour, an idea dating back to the 1700s when it was first used in the term 'the blues', referring to despondency or despair. For stress and depression, a colour from the opposite side of the colour wheel can bring additional benefits and offset blue's rather cold nature. Yellow and orange (blue's complementary opposites) are full of cheeriness, optimism and sunshine, and can help swing blue's qualities back towards positivity. Light

Blue is connected with the Throat Chakra and communication; the pure light blue of Italian skies inspired the colour to become associated with the planet Venus and its links with art and beauty and, in its purest form, spiritual aspiration and devotional love. Light blue is connected with the calm of water and the lightness of air, embodying life, refreshment, comfort and femininity. Advertisers use this colour to imply that a product is clean, safe and pure. Dark blue is connected with the Third Eye chakra and clairvoyance; its darkness has the power to stimulate thought, depth and truth. Wearing darker shades of blue give the impression of reliability, piety and dedication. Royal blue helps to restore self-confidence and to increase levels of mental and physical energy. Overall, calm, cool and collected blue is associated with thoughtfulness, peace, serenity, water and the sky above, whose pervading energy so affects all who dwell upon planet Earth.

Blue and orange, its rainbow spectrum complementary colour, as well as pink, are Libra's special LUCKY colours! The three can be worn or otherwise used together to dazzling and mesmerising effect.

LIBRA'S CHAKRA CORRESPONDENCE ★ HEART

The word 'chakra' comes from the Sanskrit and means 'wheel', disc' or 'circle'. Chakras are vitally important to your physical health, emotional wellbeing and spiritual growth, and are regarded as a complete integrated system that works holistically.

The chakras are funnel-shaped spinning energy vortexes of multi-coloured light. These swirling vortexes of energy absorb and distribute life-force, the subtle energy known as *prana*. The seven master chakras - Root, Sacral, Solar Plexus, Heart, Throat, Third Eye and Crown - lie in the centre line of the body, with the first five embedded within the spinal column. Each chakra vibrates at a different vibrational frequency and on a different note, and responds to specific life issues or 'thought forms'.

The lower body chakras deal with physical issues. As we move up the body, the chakras correspond to increasingly spiritual concerns. As a consequence, each chakra's energy vibrates at a different rate, depending on whether they govern earthbound or ethereal issues. The lower chakras have slower and denser vibrations, while the higher chakras spin at faster speeds with higher vibrations.

Because the chakras have no physical manifestation and cannot be located using any scientific instrument, they have tended to be viewed with scepticism by many Western medical professionals, a distinction they share with energy points in acupuncture and the notion of meridians. Instead, they are believed to have been sensed intuitively by many people over many centuries, and indeed people in yoga positions and in deep meditation have reported experiencing the sensation of a surge of energy rising from the base of the spine and emerging through the top of the head. Some people have even said they have seen points of blue light when their *kundalini* energy has risen from the lowest chakra to the highest, as well as experiencing a profound sense of happiness and ecstasy.

In summary, the Universal Life Force enters the body through the Crown chakra at the top of the head. As it works its way through the body, it flows through the other centres. As it spreads to the Base chakra, it is said to arouse the kundalini energy, which yogis believe sleeps in a coiled serpentine form.

The chakra associated with Libra is the fourth, or Heart chakra, which governs all matters of the heart, namely love, openness, wellbeing and compassion.

HEART CHAKRA

Location ★ Heart Region
Colour ★ Green
Concerned with ★ Love & Compassion
Gland ★ Thymus
Essential Oils ★ Clove, Lavender, Lime, Bergamot, Benzoin, Cinnamon, Elemi, Immortelle, Geranium, Grapefruit, Linden Blossom, Rose, Neroli, Mandarin, Sandalwood, Palmarosa
Animals ★ Antelope, Dove
Shape ★ Hexagram
Element ★ Air
Planet ★ Venus
Zodiac Signs ★ Libra, Taurus
Flower ★ 12-petalled Lotus
Energy State ★ Gas
Mantra ★ YAM

Positive Expression ★ Loving, accepts self and others, innate healer, generous, compassionate

Negative Expression (Blockage) ★ Selfish, envious, jealous, possessive, egotistical, melodramatic, loneliness, lack of emotional fulfilment, difficulty giving or receiving love, lack of compassion, unhealthy relationships, loving too much, unresolved sorrow

The Heart chakra is located in the region of the physical heart. Its Sanskrit name is *anahata*, and its symbol is a twelve-petal green/grey lotus flower whose centre contains a green circle and two intersecting triangles making up a six-pointed star representing balance (six is also the number of Venus, the planetary energy with which the Heart chakra is linked). This chakra blockage is especially significant because it is in the middle, uniting the upper and lower chakras. Among other things, a blockage can manifest as a lack of overall emotional fulfilment and difficulty receiving or being in a state of love. Balance in this chakra is expressed as unconditional love for ourselves and others, as well as openness to give, accept and receive compassion. It corresponds to the thymus and the cardiac nerve plexus. Crystals that can be used to cleanse and balance this chakra are mostly green and pink, such as Rose Quartz, Jade, Green Aventurine, Rhodonite, Watermelon Tourmaline, and Emerald.

LUCKY CAREER TIPS & PATHS THAT WILL MAKE YOUR BANK BALANCE & SPIRITUAL SELF SOAR

The branch of astrology known as 'vocational astrology' encompasses the areas of one's calling, career path, or ideal profession. Careers, jobs, professions and occupations can all mean different things to different people, but to simplify the definition, I refer to a vocation as one's true calling, one's authentic path, and a dynamic way of life which pays an income in some form and leads to a deep fulfilment of personal and spiritual needs. An ideal vocation will provide self-fulfilment, ego satisfaction, and feed one's inner drive to achieve what they ultimately wish to achieve, whether that be to gain recognition, wealth or approval, to travel, to learn and fulfil an inner need for knowledge, an urge to serve others in some way, or an urge to improve personal, societal or Universal conditions.

In order to gain ultimate fulfilment and self-esteem, we all need a purpose in life. Many people gain this through their work, providing the job or career they choose suits their temperament, talents and aspirations. If our professional life is unsatisfactory or disharmonious in any way, frustration, unhappiness and even despair can result. Although your whole horoscope would need to be drawn up and interpreted in order to gain more substantial, deeper insights into your ideal career and purpose, you can begin by being guided by your Sun sign, which can give you many pointers to a suitable, and therefore successful, career path. You just never know, something in the following might jump out at you and make your soul dance immediately - and hopefully all the way to the bank!

With your Sun in Libra, your greatest assets are people skills, logical reasoning, communication, and your 'gift of the gab'. You adore networking with others, smoothing over troubled waters, negotiating, mediating, and generally being on the social circuit. Out of all the zodiac signs, and aside from Leo, yours is the most likely to mix business with pleasure. Your usually fine build, graceful appearance and sense of taste and style win over many. Your ideal vocation gives you a chance to shine, work in a beautiful environment, to work with numerous interesting people, and plenty of mental stimulation.

Any work which is carried out in pleasant surroundings, and which is creative and encompasses art suits the Libran spirit. You are far better working in partnership than alone, and if you are ever thinking of going into business, you should always do so with a partner (who should take the lead in the partnership is another matter). In most cases responsibilities will be evenly shared, but your partner will have to learn to cope with your occasional over-extravagance.

You are rarely suited to any vocation that involves difficult, dirty, complicated or unpleasant working conditions.

Because Libra is the symbol of balance and equilibrium, it is appropriate that the Libran period occurs at a time of year when day and night are almost equal. Because of this principle of harmony, there are very few extremes in the Libran's character. Therefore, balance and harmony in all aspects of your life are of paramount importance, especially in the workplace where you are likely to spend a substantial amount of your time. You were certainly not born with competitive, aggressive, strident or assertive qualities, so any vocation in which there are high pressures, discord, competition or 'rat race' elements will at their best irritate your sensitive equilibrium, or at their worst exhaust you and burn you out. You intensely dislike confrontation, argument or conflict, and will do your best to avoid jobs which contain any hint of these.

As a typical Libran, you are creative on the surface, artistic and have a flair for design, or at least for knowing what looks good with what. You would therefore make an ideal: Artist, Dancer, Model, Beautician, Hairdresser, Fashion Designer, Furnisher, Decorator, Luxury Trader, Dressmaker, Salesperson, Poet, Art Dealer or Interior Designer.

Strangely enough, Librans are often interested in law and politics, but only as a means to social or public prominence - and only if it guarantees a source of income which will maintain your lifestyle and love of luxury and pleasures. You are a born strategist, usually excelling at any type of arbitration. Well-known for your tact, charm, impartiality, diplomacy, and urge for fairness and justice, you would also make a great: Diplomat, Mediator, Negotiator, Advisor, Marriage Counsellor, Legal Aid Worker, Air Steward/ess, Personnel Manager, Lawyer or Advocate.

Put bluntly, most Librans make good promoters and con artists; game playing and clever planning are your strong points. Being an Air sign, you can choose to use your intellect to manipulate and win others over. In fact, you enjoy putting other people to work on your deals, sometimes dominating and bossing them (albeit subtly) to serve your own needs. In fact, a Scorpio/Libra combination in the birth horoscope can produce a financial genius who can build a fortune by outwitting the gullible. You love having influential contacts and connections, and you will devote whatever emotional energy and resources you have to attaining status and/or wealth along your career path.

Overall, because of your innate sense of style and connection to Venus, you can be very successful in the fields of art, beauty, symmetry, luxuries, romance, graphic design, pleasure, dancing, aesthetics, and theatrical work. You could also consider working in a Boutique or Gift Shop, A Music Shop, an Art Gallery or even a Dating Agency - Librans make fantastic matchmakers! Although you are not particularly creative yourself, you are a master at applying surface attractiveness to another's original ideas - and have no issues in using this clever tactic to your advantage in any field you undertake.

LUCKY PLACES WHERE YOUR ENERGY IS HEIGHTENED

As the Air element and Sanguine humour corresponds with hot and moist conditions, warm, humid, tropical places suit your constitution, disposition and temperament. The following nations, countries and cities are also places whose vibrations are closely allied with the sign of Libra: Paris, Argentina, Korea, China, Tibet, Burma, St Lucia, The Bahamas, Uganda, Botswana, Siberia, Indo-China, Portugal (Lisbon), France (Arles), Upper Egypt, Uganda, St Pierre and Miquelon, Canada and Salvador. Costa Rica, Fiji, Equatorial Guinea, Iraq, Israel, Cuba, Saudi Arabia, Lesotho, Nigeria, Madagascar, Thailand, Japan and Austria (Vienna) are also in tune with Libran energy, as are cruise liners, art galleries, ballrooms and grand dining rooms. Visiting places which boast elegant architecture, tasteful culture, beautiful art galleries, excellent food and wine, quality shopping opportunities, being pampered and spoilt on a peaceful palm-fringed tropical island, or undertaking the ultimate pilgrimage to the aesthetically stunning and love-inspired Taj Mahal, could very well be your ticket to Libran heaven!

GEMS & CRYSTALS

"People love stones, and apparently stones love people. Like the angels they may be, they seem endlessly willing to serve the wellbeing of humans and to help us achieve our desires …Unlike people of the ancient past, we now have access to virtually the entire mineral kingdom. We have the opportunity to work like modern alchemists, combining and arranging the stones and their currents, looking for combinations and patterns that can help us enhance our inner and outer lives."

Robert Simmons, *Stones of the New Consciousness*

Each crystal and mineral of the Earth embodies different qualities, patterns or potential expressions of the Divine language, the silent whispers of the Universe. If we can accept the fact that the human body is a sophisticated, multi-faceted antenna system comprised of a crystalline matrix that is constantly transmitting and receiving all manner of energies, it could then be assumed that energy and body workers who use quartz, shells and stones, which are also crystalline materials, have the power to promote resonant interactions with the liquid 'crystal' structures found in human tissues. It could even be said that we are all made of essentially the same substances and structures, and that crystals and gemstones vibrate at varying energetic levels which can connect with our own in order to 'buzz' and dance together to make a harmonious Uni-verse both within and without.

All crystals work through vibrational balancing and by channelling energy. The magic of crystals is in their colour, which is determined by the rate at which their atoms vibrate; these vibrations can be matched to the energy given by your own body's aura. And just as light can be focused and refracted through gemstones, so too can all kinds of psychic energy, from healing energies to Divine communications.

Gemstones can help us attune to higher vibrations and bring them into our own experience and being. This theory of crystal resonance suggests that the characteristic energy patterns emanated by any stone can be transferred into the 'liquid crystal medium' of our bodies through resonance. Our bodies, being composed of these tuneable liquids, can mimic and mirror any consistent vibrational pattern with which we come into contact; we can therefore resonate with the healthful qualities of various crystals and minerals.

Crystals and precious stones have been valued throughout world cultures over many centuries for their healing virtues and capacities to imbue courage, strength, invulnerability, clairvoyance, love and numerous other qualities. Wearing gemstones is one of the simplest and most effective self-healing practices you can undertake, and wearing or carrying those stones whose vibrations correspond with the qualities you wish to embody brings their energetic currents into engagement with your body.

Over time the phenomenon of energetic integration, may be felt tangibly and your own vibrational field may internalise the stone's currents and adjust to them and effectively 'store' them, making them, eventually, a part of your own vibrational make-up. And we seem to know from the resonances we feel within our bodies when in contact with these gemstones, that crystals emanate tangible, if oft immeasurable, currents.

Crystals act as transmitters and amplifiers of your will or intentions - as long as your will or intentions are in sympathy with the crystal's energy. The mineral kingdom refers to stones, minerals and crystals and the associations and vibrations they carry. When working with stones, we are working with several different layers of spiritual energies, and although they can be regarded as inanimate 'psychic batteries', they are actually moving, vibrating masses of energy which transmit potential and power into our lives. Some crystals and stones even have receptive powers, which means they can absorb energy and retain it within until cleansed or re-programmed.

Although it is untrue that the only stones you can usefully wear are the ones astrologically matched with your Sun sign or ruling planet, those which align with your Sun sign or ruling planet are your most fortuitous and therefore strongest 'attractors' and 'amplifiers'.

Twelve oracular gemstones were described in the Bible, as the author of *Exodus* (28-15 and 17-21) knew them. Yahweh spoke to Moses about the breastplate he would have to wear to train for priesthood, and described it to him in these words: "And thou shalt make the breastplate of judgement with cunning work; ... And thou shalt set in it settings of stones, even four rows of stones; the first row shall be a sardius, a topaz, and a carbuncle. And the second row shall be an emerald, a sapphire and a diamond. And the third row an opal, an agate and an amethyst. And the fourth row a beryl, and an onyx, and a jasper; they shall be set in hold in their inclosings. And the stones shall be with the children … (all) twelve (of them)." Given that the compilers of the Bible lived during a time when astrological belief was prevalent in Babylon, it seems valid to assert that these previously named gemstones would have some astrological basis. Further, since these ancient people supposedly made correlations between each of the twelve precious stones, and one of the twelve zodiac signs, there are seven crystalline systems set down in crystallography (or the science of the laws which influence the formation, structure and geometric, physical and chemical properties of crystallised matter) as analogous with the seven traditional ruling planets of the zodiac.

However, nobody is under the rule of one planet alone. We are all in essence a complex mixture of every planet, many elements and varying aspects, depending on their positions, placements and prominence in our birth chart. Everything that goes on in the skies above us affects what is going on here on Earth, and also *within* us. Your lucky stones are to assist you to tune into your Sun sign's energy and planetary influences, but you are by no means limited to the ones listed for your sign alone. Above all, let your stones, whichever ones you choose, work for you and allow them to transport your very own unique and magical energy into the wider Universe.

> "Beautiful and strong is the material of stones, but more beautiful and much more powerful is the mystery that emanates from them."
> **Chinese Poet & Alchemist, Li Po, 8th Century A.D.**

★ CLEAR QUARTZ ★

The Master Healer ★ For All Zodiac Signs

A common, well-known and popular gem, clear quartz (sometimes known as rock crystal) is an all-purpose 'jack-of-all-trades' stone. It amplifies the magic of any work you do or wishes you make. It is connected with all the chakras and increases the power of all other crystals. Clear quartz is a deep soul cleanser, which unblocks and regulates energy and emotions on all levels. It is balancing and harmonising. In various cultures, quartz crystal is reputed to be the most powerful crystal, the 'grandfather crystal', and the 'chief of the Stone People'. Clear quartz is also considered to be the only gemstone that is modifiable to suit your needs *, as other crystals automatically contain and retain their own specific resonance or natural signature. In essence, clear quartz is the most easily programmable and the most overall healing and readily accessible crystals of the mineral kingdom, holding a unique importance in the Universe of gems. And because of its all-encompassing nature and wide-ranging healing abilities, it has zodiacal affinities with all the signs.

* To program your clear quartz crystal, simply hold it on your Third Eye chakra (between and just above the

physical eyes) and concentrate on the purpose for which you wish to use it. Be positive and receptive while you allow your crystal to fill with this energy. If you wish, you could also state the intention of the programming out loud, for example, 'I program this crystal for love / healing / meditation / abundance / protection or (insert your own word here)'. You could also run your clear quartz crystal under running water, allow it to dry naturally, then hold the stone with both hands, bring it up to your mouth and blow into it sharply three times in order to impregnate it with your own breath. Then, hold it firmly in one hand and silently invite and welcome it into your life as a friend, helper and guide.

LIBRAN & VENUSIAN LUCKY CRYSTALS, STONES & GEMS

Libra birth stones ★ Opal, Tourmaline, Sapphire

September birth stones ★ Peridot, Sapphire, Lapis Lazuli

October birth stones ★ Opal, Aquamarine, Tourmaline

Opal, Tourmaline, Sapphire (your three primary birthstones), Jade, Rose Quartz, Diamond (Venusian gems), Peridot, Sapphire, Aquamarine and Lapis Lazuli (September and October birthstones) are your luckiest stones, and one or more of these gems should be worn about your person to ensure good luck and increase your magnetism. Moonstone, Green Tourmaline, Marble, Sardonyx, Jacinth, Sunstone, Topaz, Kunzite, Mahogany Obsidian,

Ametrine, Aventurine, Chrysoprase, Citrine, Moss Agate, Amazonite, Malachite, Nephrite (Jade), Bloodstone, Kyanite, Apophyllite, Tibetan Quartz, Titanium Quartz and Green Spinel also align with Libra's energy.

CRYSTALS & THE PLANETS

All the Vedic texts agree in relating gems to planets. This verse from the *Jatax Parijat* links each gem to a planet:

> *'The ruby is the gem of the Lord of the Day (the Sun),*
> *The shining pearl is the gem of the cold Moon,*
> *Red coral is the gem of Mars,*
> *The emerald is the gem of noble Mercury,*
> *Yellow sapphire is the gem of Jupiter, instructor of gods,*
> *Diamond is the gem of Venus, instructor of demons,*
> *Blue sapphire is the gem of Saturn.'*

Each planet influences its gem, and their curative power varies according to the position of its planet in the zodiac. Ayurvedic medicine has always paid attention to these details in their healing practices, often advising people to wear their corresponding zodiacal stone as a ring or a talisman.

CRYSTALS & THE ELEMENTS

Crystals are inextricably linked to the four elements, from their original creation to their potency and use in magical rituals and healing. Formed by the combination, in varying conditions, of different physical elements, such as metals, non-metals and gases, some stones require the enormous heat generated by volcanoes or deep thermal currents to bond their molecular makeup, while others may require pressure or water sources. The effects of the four elements of Fire, Earth, Air and Water is evident in these formation processes. The heat generated by Fire, pressure from the Earth, and the chemical reactions involved in absorbing elements from the Air and Water, all demonstrate the four elements in action to produce the correct conditions and ingredients necessary for the creation of crystals, lending them each their unique qualities.

CRYSTALS & THE AIR ELEMENT

The influence of the Air element may seem less apparent as its effects often occur invisibly, but its nature and essence are very important to some crystals. The most obvious manifestation of Air is in filling spaces; such as bubbles in crystals or the hollows in geodes. Air also provides the elements necessary for chemical reactions to occur during crystal formation. As the element of the intellect, knowledge, mind and clarity, symbolically Air can also fill you with ideas and enhance mental focus. Airy crystals can therefore assist in the formulation of concepts and plans, to focus your thoughts and to make decisions.

Some Airy crystals are ★ Sapphire, Kunzite, Chalcedony, Turquoise, Lapis Lazuli, Agate, Sodalite, Opal and Rose Quartz.

THE CRYSTALLINE SYSTEM OF YOUR RULING PLANET VENUS

Associated with your ruling planet Venus, are Emerald, Pink Coral, Lapis Lazuli, Agate, Beryl, Amazonite, Albite, Pearl, Aquamarine and Light Sapphire. This is the sixth crystalline system, known as triclinical, that is having a parallelepiped on a diamond-shaped base. The stone which perhaps represents this system best, the Amazonite, or aluminium and potassium double silicate, is a brilliant example of it. Analogous with Venus, the triclinical Amazonite had qualities of bringing hope and love to those who wore it.

VENUS'S GEMSTONE ASSOCIATION

★ **Diamond** ★ Universally considered the greatest of stones, the diamond has been revered throughout the ages for its beauty and strength. The Ancient Greeks believed that diamonds were actually splinters of stars that had fallen to Earth, and it was thought by some they were the tears of the gods. Diamond is pure crystallised carbon and is known as the ruler of the mineral kingdom, due to its hardwearing qualities, hardness and sheer brilliance. Diamond is the purest substance in nature and one of the hardest (10 out of 10 on the Mohs scale). The word 'diamond' has its origin in the Greek word 'adamas', which means unconquerable. Mined for over 4,000 years, ancient civilisations discovered that this amazing gem could cut any other stone. The diamond is known universally as a token of love; quite simply, it is the ultimate symbol of purity. This luminously brilliant gem, through its renowned purity and durability, offers incomparable proof of total perfection expressed in a single element. Its pure white light can help to bring your life into a cohesive whole, the first step in using your power to optimum effect. It bonds relationships, is said to enhance the love of a husband to his wife, brings love and clarity into a partnership, and is seen as a sign of commitment and faithfulness. Psychologically, this precious gem imparts a sense of fearlessness, fortitude and invincibility, for diamonds are unbreakable in every sense of the word. Diamond is also an amplifier of any energy with which it comes into contact, therefore should only be used for positive spells and magic, and is one of the few stones that never needs recharging or cleansing; in fact, it increases the energy of whatever it comes into contact with and is very effective when used with other crystals for healing as it enhances and draws out their power.

Like the clear quartz, it is a master healer which accelerates the spiritual development of its wearer. As an amplifier of energy, the merciless light of diamond will highlight anything that is negative and requires transformation. Diamond has been a symbol for wealth for thousands of years and is one of the stones of manifestation, with the ability to attract abundance; the larger the diamond, the more abundance will be drawn to the requester. Diamond helps to clear emotional and mental pain, alleviates fear and brings about new beginnings. It also provides a link between the intellect and the higher mind, aiding clarity and enlightenment of mind. On a spiritual level, it allows one's soul light to shine out, cleansing the aura of anything shrouding the inner light, and reminds you of your soul's aspirations; it activates the Crown chakra, linking it to the 'Divine light'. Indeed, clear crystals such as diamond will interact with your energy field by raising your vibration through clearing away any cloudiness or blockages within your subtle bodies. With it may be worn a bloodstone, another Arien gemstone, when the beneficent influence of the diamond will be greatly increased. A highly creative stone, stimulating imagination and inventiveness, and aiding spiritual evolution.

LIBRA'S FEATURE CRYSTAL ★ OPAL

This is a beautiful and delicate stone with a fine vibration, reminding us of the wondrous unfolding of the Divine Universe. As it contains all the colours of the other stones, it can be used to amplify all other stones' energies. Unlike most other gemstones, opal is not crystalline in form, but rather is defined as a mineraloid. It is an amorphous silica variety of quartz, is comparatively soft, and owes its beauty to the wonderful play of colour from its surface. The mineral is formed from the shells or skeletons of very tiny plant and animal organisms, and occurs in many different colours and varieties, such as fire opal, girasol quartz, moss opal, milk opal, precious opal and resin opal, among others. Bringing miraculous order to a vast array of patterns and colours, the opal unites heaven and Earth in a union of water and fire. The characteristically iridescent, rainbow hues of the gem are caused by irregular refraction of light from its surface, which is traversed by innumerable tiny cracks. In the process of its formation, the surface becomes covered by these cracks, and these crevices become filled in with a substance containing more or less water than the surrounding surface. A great irregularity and refraction and a play of colour varies according to the angle from which the gem is viewed: blue, perhaps when looked at in one direction, yellow or crimson if we view it from another.

Known as the Queen of Gems, opal is one of the most beautiful stones and has been highly prized for thousands of years. Opals have always generated strong passions, according to the folklore of many cultures. In Ancient Egypt and Babylon, opals were considered a powerful healing gem, combining the qualities of fire and water, and were said to bring good luck. Opal was also sacred to medieval England, Greece and some Arabic societies. Opal is said to improve vitality by magnifying energy, enhance one's self-image, improve one's fortune or luck, have protective powers, stimulate cosmic consciousness and induce psychic visions. It is considered capable of opening up the Third Eye and Crown chakras, and above other minerals is used by many mystics to lead them into supernatural and otherworldly realms. Absorbent and reflective, on a spiritual level opal picks up thoughts and feelings, amplifies them, and returns them to Source. A protective and karmic stone, it teaches that what you put out comes back. An excellent aid for transformation, opal enhances self-worth and helps you understand your full potential. It stimulates originality and dynamic creativity, and encourages an interest in the arts. Opal is also associated with desire and eroticism, love and passion; it is a seductive stone that intensifies emotional states and dissolves inhibitions. It can also help you gain access to your true self, magnifying your personality traits and bringing them to the surface for healing. Overall, opal will work well with the emotional, mental, spiritual and etheric bodies. It can provide a much-needed burst of energy, boost self-confidence, enhance creativity and intuition, help release anger, and connect one to the Higher Self. Opal contains more water than any other mineral, up to 21 per cent, and is porous, so it should not be immersed in water or brought into contact with oils, as these may harm or destroy it.

LIBRAN POWER CRYSTALS

Around six thousand years ago, in ancient Mesopotamia, the Sumerians started studying precious stones and minerals, as well as the stars, with a view of improving their lives in many ways by probing the secrets and mysteries of the Universe. Their esoteric interests and knowledge were such that they began to grasp the general connections between the Earth and the heavens, or the Solar system as they knew it, and the functions of stones and minerals as a link between the two. Their method of making these connections was by colour (for example the Sun was allocated all yellow stones), as well as other spiritual links. The gemstones listed for the portion of your zodiac sign are given their status as your 'power crystals' due to the links that can be made between your primary planetary ruler/s and your mutable planetary ruler (listed last), and each stone's particular colour, chemical and mineral compositions, healing properties, and the number they are given (based on the Mohs scale of hardness: for example, diamond scores a perfect 10 out of 10), all of which combine to align with your planetary rulers. Working mindfully with your planet's special crystals is one way you can increase the flow of power and magic into your life.

POWER CRYSTALS FOR FIRST HALF LIBRANS ★ (22 September t- 6 October)

Influenced by Venus and Uranus

Spinel, White Topaz, Kyanite, Dioptase, Tsavorite, Wavellite

★ **SPINEL** ★ Spinel is a chameleon among jewels, coming in a wider range of tints than any other variety of stone. It is rarer than ruby or sapphire, with which it is often found, and it has a similar hardness to these two, a considerable 7.5 to 8 (the ancients classified the red spinel as a 'female ruby'). Spinel is a beautiful crystal, coming in colours of white, red, violet, black, green, blue, brown, orange, yellow and colourless. Connected with energy renewal, it opens the chakras and facilitates movement of kundalini energy up the spine, offering encouragement in challenging circumstances. It has rejuvenating and restorative properties, and enhances the positive aspects of one's character. Spinels come in several hues, and for Librans the best are the clear, blue and dark green types. Colourless, or clear, spinel stimulates mysticism and communication with higher realms. It links the chakras of the physical body with the Crown chakra of the etheric body, facilitating enlightenment and visionary experiences. The blue spinel stimulates communication and channelling, and is aligned with and opens the Throat chakra. Green spinel stimulates love, kindness and compassion, and opens and is connected with the Heart chakra. Overall, spinel is a hardwearing stone and occurs in the same crystal systems as the diamond. The planets Uranus and Venus are co-rulers of this stone, with the result that spinel, on the spiritual plane, is effectively directed towards promoting general idealism through harmony, originality, creativity and in particular the making of music.

★ **KYANITE** ★ Kyanite, also called disthene, is an indigo, translucent blue, white, grey, yellow, black or green-blue stone, which is aligned with the Crown, Third Eye and Throat chakras. Kyanite is the perfect example of symmetrical elegance, and habitually reminiscent of bluish-grey skies, it has a soft luminosity glowing from its depths. Kyanite grows in flat blade crystals that often have striations (parallel scratches or grooves) along their length, giving this crystal a focused swift action quality that is augmented by these streaks. Kyanite's grooves allow the crystal to move energy quickly between the chakra linkage points, which releases energy blocks, ties, 'hooks' and ensnarement imposed upon one's spirit by other people or negative situations. Kyanite restores one's energy balance and integrates the body's forces. With conscious attunement it aligns all the chakras and activates their linkage points, balancing and strengthening the subtle bodies. In healing, it stabilises the biomagnetic field after clearing and transformation. Kyanite strengthens the Throat chakra and its life-force energy can open the way for spiritual healing. It encourages self-expression and speaking one's truth, cutting through ignorance, fears and blockages. It can also facilitate astral or interdimensional travel, enhance creative expression and is particularly useful for meditation, especially if you are having trouble relaxing or clearing the mind. Kyanite transforms negative thought patterns and opens up the Crown chakra to assist in connecting to your higher self. Calming and tranquillising, this stone promotes clarity and understanding, and with its ability to tune into the 'causal' level, this stone can help spiritual energy manifest in thought. Kyanite's metaphysical name is 'the sword of truth'. As the seeker of truth it enhances psychic abilities, inner guidance and intuition, and connects the higher mind to the highest frequencies.

★ **DIOPTASE** ★ Dioptase often comes in a glittering cluster of hypnotic green crystals more vibrant than any emerald. In fact, this rare and expensive stone rivals the emerald in the beauty of its colouring and in its holistic powers. One of the most highly spiritual stones, dioptase brings a heightened state of awareness, emotional stability, and the gift of raised consciousness to its wearer. Not suitable for cutting due to its brittle nature, this transparent gem is a powerful healer for the heart and opens the higher Heart chakra. Its beautiful deep-green or emerald green colouring raises the functioning of all the chakras, especially the Heart, and has a dramatic effect on the human energy field, facilitating great spiritual attunement. Dioptase appears in brilliant small crystals which sit on a host rock, usually on a matrix, and if found in pendant form (many a magnificent rich-green pendant has been fashioned around a nest of natural dioptase crystals), this jewel should be worn mid-chest where it can emanate its most powerful benefits. Dioptase is a strong mental cleanser and detoxifier, acting as a bridge to emotional healing and dissolving and easing the pain associated with abandonment, heartache, grief, betrayal and sorrow. As such, dioptase teaches that ultimately pain and difficulty in a relationship is a reflection of an inner separation from the *self*. It can repair that link and draw in love at all levels, filling in emotional 'black holes', clearing away old perceptions and notions of how love should be, and bringing in a new vibration of love. Dioptase supports a more positive attitude to life and overcomes any sense of lack. It can also enable the fulfilling of one's innate potential and indicates direction when you are unsure of what to do next. Dioptase encourages living in the present moment, and paradoxically also activates past-life memories. It can be programmed for use with affirmations that enhance self-esteem and self-worth. Aligning both the physical and etheric bodies, it is also excellent for cellular regeneration and healing. Spiritually, dioptase can raise awareness of inner riches by enhancing spiritual and psychic attunement and receptivity, sharpening ESP faculties, and promoting guidance from higher planes when placed upon the Third Eye.

POWER CRYSTALS FOR SECOND HALF LIBRANS ★ (7 - 22 October)

Influenced by Venus and Mercury

Blue Sapphire, Sillimanite, Green Jadeite, Adamite on Limonite, Ilmenite

★ **BLUE SAPPHIRE** ★ The hardest crystal after diamond, sapphire has long held a reputation for its amazing spiritual as well as physical properties. A variety of the mineral corundum, it is a symbol of ultimate truth and imminent justice. Sapphire is found in a variety of colours, including blue, yellow, white, black, purple and green - but the blue variety is probably the best known. Sapphire is known as the wisdom stone, each colour having its own particular wisdom, with all hues bringing prosperity and attracting gifts of all kinds. Its name is derived from the Sanskrit word *Sani*, which means Saturn. Sapphire has always been associated with love, fidelity, joy, prosperity, the heavens and the angels. In Vedic astrology, gemstones such as the blue and yellow sapphires are believed to work through physiochemical and electrochemical means. Blue sapphire is believed to encourage altruism and generosity, to stimulate the imagination and curiosity, and in ancient times had the reputation of winning those who wore it numerous friendships. Especially prized by the ancient Greeks and appearing throughout their mythology, those who wished to put a question to the famous Delphic Oracle had to wear a sapphire. There are many legends surrounding this luminous blue stone: The Ten Commandments were said to be written on tablets of sapphire, and King Solomon was believed to have used one to commune with God. An old Persian myth tells that the Earth sat on a giant sapphire which gave the sky its brilliant blue colour. In Buddhism, sapphire is known as the 'stone of the stones' because of its connection with the qualities of devotion, happiness, spiritual enlightenment and tranquillity. Due to its highly soothing and balancing effect, sapphire is beneficial for treating nervous conditions such as panic attacks, anxiety and stress. Labelled the 'Gem of the Heavens', sapphire was believed to bestow its wearer with strengthened vision, including prophetic visions of the future. It is a symbol of truth and constancy. The least passionate of stones, the dark blue sapphire acts directly on the intellect and perhaps for that very reason is often the subconscious choice for those who wish to fall back on the reassurance of status and wealth rather than emotions. Because blue sapphire has a particular affinity for the Throat chakra, it prompts you to express your truth and beliefs. As well as encouraging communication, it is excellent for improving mental focus and clarity. Blue sapphire has a calming and balancing effect on emotions and may also be used to open up the Crown and Third Eye chakras to the angelic realms. Some sapphires are believed to be record-keepers and may aid you to access the knowledge of ancient civilisations when dreaming, 'journeying' or meditating. Use it to connect to your spirit guides and teachers and for interdimensional communication, as it connects mind, body and spirit. Overall, blue sapphire encourages you to reach for the stars, speak your truth, and stay on your rightful spiritual path.

★ **GREEN JADEITE** ★ Two crystals are commonly known as jade by the gem trade: jadeite and nephrite. Although nephrite and jadeite are two distinct minerals with differing holistic values, they do share many similarities. Jadeite was recognised as a separate mineral in 1863 by a French chemist, who analysed two separate specimens from China and found them to be different minerals. Since nephrite was firmly established, he called the second specimen jadeite. Jadeite's colours range through green, white, pink, black, yellow and mauve, with green being probably the most well-known. The most sought-after colouring is an intense apple green, an eye-catching, extremely rare and highly attractive gem also known as Imperial Jade. Jade brings peace through serenity and cleanses the energy centres. Green jade strengthens the Heart chakra and can be used to harmonise dysfunctional relationships. It calms the nervous system and channels passion in constructive ways. It increases love and nurturing and symbolises harmony, purity, protection, good luck and friendship. It is a serenity stone and is excellent for healing conditions associated with stress and feelings of overwhelming obligation. A wonderful ally in healing others, jade is a good stone for those who are beginner healers or who wish to give their healing skills an added boost. The ancients considered jade a sacred stone and it was traditionally worn as a stone of good fortune. On a spiritual level jade has an affinity for the Heart chakra and it harmonises relationships, encourages compassion and the establishment of strong bonds, and balances the nervous system, dispelling moods swings and calming anger and irritability. It brings composure when it is worn, carried or used, and instils wisdom, promotes feelings of tranquillity, cleanses feelings and stabilises the temperament. Jade has a long history of being used to attract wealth and prosperity due to its associations with royalty. Chinese business people have extensively used jade to attract new business and promote worthy causes and ventures. Placing a piece of jade in your work space is beloved to attract wealth, and enhance calm and harmony in the work environment. Used with other stones or on its own, it is traditionally believed to generate abundance and attract good fortune in all areas of life. Jade is also a useful 'dream' stone; placed under your pillow, it encourages insightful dreams and will help you to not only remember your dreams, but also to interpret them. In addition, as a stone of wisdom, it assists us to reach decisions about meaningful things. Spiritually, jade encourages you to become who you really are. Awakening hidden knowledge within yourself, it assists in recognising yourself as a spiritual being on a human journey. A profoundly spiritual stone, jade encourages you to recognise that you have access to much wider powers and dimensions than can be physically seen, and as such motivates you to become all that you can be. It can also assist your understanding of any blocks which may be hindering the manifestation or progress of your goals. Jade has the wonderful attribute of dispelling all negativity and indeed has been considered a sacred stone by various cultures for many centuries. The Chinese call jadeite 'Yu Shih' meaning Yu stone, believing it to contain all five cardinal virtues needed for a happy existence: modesty, courage, charity, justice and wisdom. Maori greenstone jade is a master healer and powerful manifestor.

YOUR LUCKY NUMBERS

Your lucky numbers are ★ 6 for Libra ^ & 6 for Venus (also, see 'Lucky Magic Square of Venus')

LUCKY MAGIC SQUARE OF VENUS

In Western occult tradition, each planet has traditionally been associated with a series of numbers and particular arrangements of those numbers. One such method of numerological organisation is the magic square. Magic squares date back to ancient times, appearing in China about 3,000 years ago. The first Chinese square is seen in the scroll of the river Lo - the Lo-Shu, a scroll believed to have been created by Fuh-Hi, the mythical founder of Chinese civilisation. Certain squares came to be linked with the planets; these associations came from the Babylonians. Each *kamea*, or magic square, is linked with a particular planet, and each of the squares has a *seal*, which is the geometric pattern created by following the numbers in order of their value. This pattern touches upon all the numbers of the square and the seal is used to represent the entire square. An intelligence and a spirit are also associated with each kamea, derived from the key numbers contained within it, using a Hebrew form of numerology. This intelligence is viewed as an inspiring, guiding and informing entity.

The 'Magic Square of Venus ' is divided into 49 cells, or squares, seven across and seven down. Each square contains a number between 1 and 49. The sum of the numbers in the vertical, horizontal and diagonal lines is a constant of 175. The total of these numbers is 1225. Therefore, the numbers 7, 49, 175 and 1225 are also assigned to Venus.

YOUR NUMEROLOGY NUMBER & LUCKY SUN SIGN NUMBERS

"Everything that exists has a vibration. The vibration of sound, music, colour, matter, even our words, thoughts, and names show form. All vibration is measurable. To measure we need numbers. Numbers are the basis of all. Numbers are the key to all mysteries."
Shirley Blackwell Lawrence, *Behind Numerology*

Numerology is essentially the metaphysical * 'science' of numbers. The use of numbers in magic is its cornerstone of power. The ancient Greek philosopher and mathematician Pythagoras, born around 590 BC, embarked on a thirty-year spiritual quest studying with important religious and esoteric teachers and healers to find the mystery of 'The Hidden Light', and came to see mankind as living in three worlds: the natural, the human and the Divine. He asserted that all things can be expressed in numerical terms, because they are ultimately reducible to numbers. Pythagoras stated that "Numbers are the first things of all of Nature" and followed the theory that "Nothing can exist without numbers."

Many believe that numbers have an arcane, mystical relationship with words, and with inanimate and animate objects; the interpretations that arose from these relationships date back to a time when the dawning intelligence of primitive man first visualised the meaning of numbers and associated it with spiritual significance. Numerology is the science of the exploration of this relationship in order to discover hidden meanings, forecast the future or interpret the character of a person. In its more modern applications, a series of figures which correspond to an individual's name and date of birth are calculated, and practitioners believe one's prospects, fortune and character can be deciphered from the results ^.

So what is numerology and how does one use it? Everything in the Universe has a vibrational frequency, an energy, a force, all vibrating at various rates, and we as humans are no exception, the difference between one person and another is their rate of vibration. This force or energy is constantly in motion and changing, and we can even 'tune into' and feel our vibrations if we are still for long enough.

Along with letters, sounds, colours, crystals, and many other things, it is believed that numbers also have vibrations, and when we are able to familiarise ourselves with our own numerical frequencies, we can use this familiarity to add power and magic to our lives. The numbers of our birth date, the letters of our names, and the numbers of our Sun sign and ruling planets, all have a unique vibrational frequency, and herein lies the key to understanding our self and our journey through life. Numerology refers to the knowledge contained within the numbers of our birth date and our name, and this is our own personal magic which can greatly assist us through life.

* Metaphysics is the study of those sciences that extend beyond the physical or tangible

HOW TO FIND YOUR NUMEROLOGY NUMBER

^ Your Sun sign's number was added up according to the principle of corresponding a number with a letter, for example 1=A, 2=B, 3=C and so on in sequence and up to 9=I, then beginning again at number 1 for the next letter J and following this same sequence. Following this system, the sum of the letters in Libra vibrates to the number 6.

Your personal numerology number is determined by adding up all the numbers in your birth date until they reach a two-digit figure. The two resulting numbers are then added together again to form a single digit, which is your personal numerology number. For example, someone born on 3 February 1983, would add the digits 3 + 2 + 1 + 9 + 8 + 3 = 26 = (reduced to two digits) 8. So that person's personal numerology birth number is 8.

Each primary number or birth number from 1 to 9 has a specific meaning and is governed by a planetary force. The principle of numerology reduces all numbers down to the following: 1 to 9, and 10, 11, 13 and 22 *. The last four numbers only apply to people specially concerned with the occult and spiritualism - and can be studied at greater length through other sources if so desired - and can in any case be reduced further to a single digit if preferred.

Your birth number contains a unique power, and therein lie your strengths, shortcomings and opportunities. It is beyond the scope of this book to outline your individual numerology number possibilities, so for the purposes of astrological applications, I have only included your Sun sign and ruling planet's special numbers.

* The numbers 10 and 13, and the master numbers 11 and 22, can be further reduced to one digit if so desired; however, they can be interpreted as they are without further reduction. The choice is personal.

BASIC MEANINGS & KEYWORDS

1 ★ Sun. Masculine influence, beginnings, independence, inventiveness, originality, leadership, exploration, innovation, ambition
2 ★ Moon. Feminine influence, cooperation, partnership, tact, diplomacy, harmony, unity, emotions, imagination, adaptability
3 ★ Jupiter. Communication, expression, youthfulness, self-confidence, creativity, inspiration, optimism, curiosity
4 ★ Uranus. Order, form, security, stability, patience, restriction, work, values, practicality
5 ★ Mercury. Freedom, inconsistency, change, variety, travel, activity, learned
6 ★ Venus. Love, home, family, sense of duty, responsibility, marriage, justice, nurturing, balance, gentleness, peace, friendship

7 ★ Neptune. Analysis, wisdom, mystical, spiritual, solitude, precision, research, integrity, mystery, psychic perceptions

8 ★ Saturn. Money, power, success, organisation, hard work, business, health, purpose, control, authority, mastery

9 ★ Mars. Completion, endings, Universal, service, humanity, philanthropy, loyalty

10 ★ Fortunate, creative, vibrant, stable, optimistic, original, successful, determined, individualistic

11 ★ Master number. Prophecies, inspiration, moral courage, missionary, long-suffering, foolhardiness, enlightenment, invention

13 ★ Misunderstood, fearful, changeable, interested in the occult, fatalistic, flexible, sacred, beguiling

22 ★ Master number. Powerful, successful, idealistic, attracted to the occult, creative, wise, successful, masterful, spiritually understanding

★ THE NUMBER 6 – FOR LIBRA & VENUS ★

Names ★ Sextile, Hexad, Senary, Sextet, Sextuple, Hexagon

Arithmomantic connections with the letters of the alphabet ★ F, O and X

Ruled by Venus, the number 6 is a loving, stable and harmonious vibration. A perfect number because it is the sum of its factors (1, 2, 3), 6 is balanced, and is associated with family love and domesticity. Number 6 people are very reliable and trustworthy, but may be obstinate. The Hexagon, the number 6 or the Hexad is represented geometrically as a 6-sided, balanced figure. It is also symbolised by two intersecting triangles known as the Seal of Solomon. Considered a sacred number to some religions who believe that the world was created in 6 days, as such the double triangle was and is frequently carved in stone or painted on windows in old monasteries and churches. In nature we find many examples of the hexagonal in the form of crystals, which are a complete and very comprehensive class in themselves. On the whole, the Hexas has always been considered one of the happiest numbers, since it represents perfect harmony and completion. As well, 6 has long been regarded as a particularly lucky number, with great balance. It possesses an extremely harmonious nature, associated with love, service and responsibility. Symbolised by the 6-pointed star, its colours are pale blues, turquoises, greens and indigo. It denotes equilibrium, and the six-pointed star is comprised of two triangles, one pointing upwards towards the 'spirit' or heavens, and the other pointing down towards the body or Earth, symbolising balance between them. This association with balance is partly due to the qualities of a cube, a six-sided figure which has shown great stability whichever way up it appears. The cube also displays an equal face in all four directions, plus a face pointing towards the heavens, the so-called fifth or esoteric dimension. Each side of the die is numbered, with six the highest and therefore the most fortuitous of the numbers. Number 6 promises fame and the gifts of prophesy to its sympathetic and compassionate subjects who may also suffer from anxiety, jealousy or a quick temper. Carrying the vibe of Venus, it is the number of family, comfort, graciousness and beauty but also represents duty and responsibility. People who wish for a steady way of life, and who enjoy being of service to others will particularly benefit. However, there could be a danger that too much is expected by kith and kin which can lead to tension. Yet 6 is the number of the voice, and therefore highly beneficial for anyone interested in a singing career. They can also be over-protective, unwilling to change, anxious, worrisome, suspicious, superficial, possessive, cynical and emotionally unstable. They are responsible, conventional, self-sacrificing, compassionate, protective, loyal, domestic, fair, idealistic with a flair for teaching and healing. The planet Venus governs devotion in love, but number 6 people are more romantic than sensual. Number 6s are born to sing, so a musical path is well suited to these types. You have a great love of beauty, are usually attractive and have a greater ability to make friends than any other number. Despite a loathing of any kind of discord, you can be quite a stubborn fighter. Your luckiest day is Friday.

Alchemy ★ Six is the principle of reconciliation. In alchemy, it represents the union of fire and water, brought into a harmonious relationship. Six is shown as a hexagon, or a six-pointed star made up of two interlaced triangles, which point above and below, symbolising unity between heaven and Earth.

LUCKY 'MAGIC HOURS' OR 'TIME UNITS'

One rule of magic, luck and power, as already outlined elsewhere in this book, can be found within the well-known phrase, "As above, so below." From the most ancient times, the planets were said to rule Earthly destinies and powers. Days of the week were named after the seven planets which were the only ones then known: Sun Day, Moon Day, Mars Day (French: Mardi), Mercury Day (French: Mercredi), Jove Day (French: Jeudi), Venus Day (French: Vendredi) and Saturn Day.

The planetary hours are based on an ancient astrological system, the Chaldean order of the planets. The Chaldean order indicates the relative orbital velocity of the planets, and from a heliocentric (helios = The Sun) perspective, this sequence also indicates the relative distance of the planets from the Sun (the Sun switching places with the Earth in this sequence), and the distance of the Moon from the Earth.

Before an action is taken in daily life, or a transaction undertaken, for instance, it is possible to choose the appropriate day and hour that will provide the greatest chances of success. By studying the planetary hours system, you will discover which actions are propitious to which of the seven planets or 'star-gods' and at what time it would be advisable to undertake them.

The planetary hours system uses this Chaldean order to divide time, and each planetary hour of the planetary day is ruled by a different planet. The order is repeated, starting with the slowest: Saturn - then, Jupiter, Mars, Sun, Venus, Mercury, Moon, then back to Saturn, Jupiter, Mars, etc., ad infinitum. The planet that rules the first hour of the day is also the ruler of that whole day and gives the day its name. So the first hour of Saturday is ruled by Saturn, the first hour of Sunday by the Sun, and so on. It is important, for the purposes of using specific planetary energies for our magic and wishes, to note that planetary hours are not considered the same length as our normal timekeeping slots of sixty minutes. Each day is split into time periods, day time and night time, beginning at around sunrise and sunset respectively. These two time periods are each divided into twelve equal-length hours, which are the planetary hours. So the planetary hours of the day and the planetary hours of the night will be of different lengths, except during the equinoxes when light and darkness are balanced.

In sequence, the Sun, Moon and the five visible planets each exerts its own special influence over a twenty-four-hour period. I like to call your planet's special day and hour the 'Magic Hour'.

Magic rituals to draw luck and love to you should be conducted at astrologically correct times and with the appropriate instruments, tools, cards, herbs, flowers, oils and plants which are linked with the ruling planet. For example, a love ritual, spell or potion demands a concoction of any or all of the above ruled by Venus. Do not underestimate rulerships, for they wield an unseen power that can help make our dreams, big and small, come true.

Further, as specific hours of each day are ruled by certain planets, if you are really serious about attracting some power, luck or magic into your life, it is imperative that you wish, pray or ask at the most opportune times for your Sun sign. There are two methods you can use for fine tuning your magical workings. The first method is to perform your spell, ritual or wishing on the day your Sun sign's ruling planet during the planetary hour that signifies the essence of what you are asking for (e.g. A Libran who is looking for a career change might perform a career-seeking ritual on a Friday, during a Saturn-ruled planetary hour [Saturn is the planet concerned with careers]. Alternatively, if you wish to summon the power of your Sun sign's own ruling planet, then that same Libran might perform their career-seeking ritual on a Saturday (ruled by Saturn) during Venus's planetary hour.)

The nature of that which you are asking for, such as love, travel opportunities, money, career guidance, protection or friendship for example, should always be considered when choosing the day or hour during which your magic will be heightened.

The answer to the question why are there seven days in a week, is a very important one to know in unravelling the secret of your Magic Hours. Ancient people recognised the supreme importance of the seven heavenly spheres, which comprised those which could be seen by the naked eye: The Sun, Moon, Mercury, Venus, Mars, Jupiter and Saturn. They then named each of the seven days of the week after one of those spheres and assigned that planetary 'ruler' to one day of the week. As viewed from Earth, these seven spheres appear to move at varying speeds, and the ancients used this factor to arrange them in order of varying speed. If you intend to use your Magic Hours to attract wonderful things, you must memorise that sequence because it is what forms the basis of the whole system.

Whenever you intend to use your Magic Hours or, perhaps more accurately, Magic *Time Units*, it is important to find out the exact time of sunrise for the area in which you live, as sunrise marks the time when your planet's magic is at its most powerful on its specific day. So, at sunrise on Sunday, the Sun rules the hour following the sunrise, the Moon rules the first hour following sunrise on a Monday, and through the week the pattern is repeated, with each day's ruling planet beginning the cycle in that first hour after dawn. It is logical then, that the rest of the planets, in sequence, follow on with one planet per hour for that day thereafter for the rest of the 24-hour cycle, creating a Magic Hour or Time Unit for each planet throughout the day and night, depending on which planet rules that particular day and is therefore the first in line.

If you wish to explore the idea in more depth, it is worth noting first and foremost that each day contains twenty-four hours, but, depending on the season, day and night will be of varying lengths. In summer, daylight is longer than darkness, whereas the reverse applies in winter. During autumn and spring, day and night are usually about equal. Therefore, although a complete day always contains twenty-four hours, there are not always twelve hours between sunrise and sunset and another twelve hours between sundown and the following sunrise. So, depending on the season (and location), a time unit may be shorter than one hour, longer than one hour, or equal to one hour. So whenever you intend to use your Magic Time Units, it is important to find out the exact time of sunrise and sunset for the area in which you live. The next step is to divide the amount of day time (if day when you wish to work your 'magic', otherwise the same following theory applies to night time) into twelve equal sections by calculating the number of hours and minutes between sunrise and sunset and divide by twelve. An example is if the Sun rises at 6.27 a.m. and sets at 5.49 p.m., the amount of time contained in this day is eleven hours and twenty-two minutes. Convert this total into minutes (682) and then divide that figure by twelve (57). Therefore, each of the twelve daylight time units will be 57 minutes on that day.

Although this wonderful method of using astrology is very ancient, it may be completely new to you. You are in for a pleasant surprise though, because if you are willing to delve into a little research and put the system to the test, rich rewards are in store for you!

YOUR LUCKY DAY ★ FRIDAY

Planet ★ Venus
Basic Energy ★ Socialisation
Basic Magic ★ Love, Friendships, Pleasure, Art, Beauty
Element ★ Air
Colour ★ Green
Energy Keywords ★ Affection, Gentleness, Attraction, Diplomacy, Love, Art, Harmony, Appreciation, Sociability, Consideration, Beauty, Construction, Devotion, Cooperation, Femininity, Romance, Flirtiness

Friday is the day of Venus, your planetary ruler. In commonly used calendars, Friday is the sixth day of the week, though in others it is the fifth. The English name is derived from Old English *Frigedaeg*, a result of an old convention associating the goddess Frigg with the goddess Venus, with whom the day is associated. Good Friday, the day before Easter that commemorates the crucifixion of Jesus, Black Friday, referring to several historical disasters that happened on a Friday, Friday the 13th, and Casual Friday, a relaxation of dress codes adopted in some corporations, are some well-known examples with which Venus's day is associated.

Venus is the goddess often associated with love, but she rules over all kinds of partnerships, and harmony, balance, beauty and aesthetics generally. If you wish to change your image or purchase a work of art for your environment, then Venus can help.

In the folk rhyme 'Monday's Child', 'Friday's child is loving and giving'. It is a day of Love, Relationships, Business Partnerships, Marriage, Beauty, Harmony, Balance, Indulgence, Luxury and Pampering, and an opportune time for making wishes or working magic involving love, relationships, beauty, social gatherings, art, style and romance.

VENUS'S MAGIC TIME UNITS
(BASED ON THE PLANETARY HOURS)
FOR EACH DAY OF THE WEEK

SATURDAY ★ Fifth and Twelfth time units after sunrise
SUNDAY ★ Second and Ninth time units after sunrise
MONDAY ★ Sixth time unit after sunrise
TUESDAY ★ Third and Tenth time units after sunrise
WEDNESDAY ★ Seventh time unit after sunrise
THURSDAY ★ Fourth and Eleventh time units after sunrise
FRIDAY ★ First and Eighth time units after sunrise **

Choose the Hour/s of Venus for any transaction, exchange, activity, initiative, venture or wish which involves love, romance, partnerships, business negotiations, pleasure, leisure, good company, style, art, fast cash, friendships, parties, gatherings, marriage harmony and relationships.

** Please note that for the purposes of simplification, the information regarding 'Venus's Magic Time Units' is a very diluted and simplified version of using magical times to your advantage. These hours cover only daylight hours, or the first twelve hours after sunrise, and do not take into account magical times after sunset or throughout the night.

'Hours' is also a deceptive term, as most 'time periods' used in this system are less than an hour, but for the purposes of simplifying the technique, I refer to them as Magic Hours (to keep with the tradition of the term 'planetary hours') rather than magic 'time units', which is what they really are. Should you wish to do further research on your ruling planet's most powerful time units, or require further information about the planet/s from which you are seeking 'energy' from in order to assist your wish-making, other sources may provide you with more comprehensive and detailed information.

A LITTLE NEW MOON / MAGICAL TIME UNIT WISH RITUAL

Step 1 ~ Choose the Magical Hour and/or day that matches your intentions. The first dawn hour of Sunday, ruled by the Sun, is a great time for all-purpose magic, success, joy, abundance, prosperity, bliss, personal power & all-round expansion.

Step 2 ~ Write out a little wish list with the appropriate coloured pen on the colour paper which corresponds to your desire.

Step 3 ~ Choose a small stone of your choosing that is connected to your wish (or a number of stones, that are perhaps linked with your planetary ruler's number, for example 6 for Venus).

Step 4 ~ Find a nice patch of soil in your garden or any special place to you, dig into it, affirm your wish in your mind, place the crystal/s and piece of paper in the hole, then place a plant on top of the crystal/s and wish list.

Step 5 ~ Fill the soil back in over the roots of the plant and feed it with a little water out of a magical vessel (a small genie bottle would be ideal).

Step 6 ~ Thank the Earth, the Universe and the Sun (or whatever planet you are summoning the power from) for bringing forth your desires.

Step 7 ~ Repeat all day long: "Thank You, Thank You, Thank You!"

Step 8 ~ Watch your plant - and your wish - grow bigger and bigger as time goes on!

YOUR LUCKY CHARM/TALISMANS

The following are three 'materials' or talismanic symbols from which to make your lucky charms, and the planetary energy under which to do it, corresponding with your Sun sign:

LIBRA ★ Opal, Scales, Copper, Venus

"When any star ascends fortunately, take a stone and
herb that are under that star, make a ring of
the metal that is congruous therewith, and in that fix
the stone with the herb under it."
Henry Cornelius Agrippa, *On Occult Philosophy*

Charms, talismans and amulets are among the oldest forms of magic. A charm or talisman is a symbol, often used to communicate a thought, prayer or wish to, or to make a connection with the Divine. It is usually in the form of an object, which has been imbued with mysterious and magical powers. A charm may be as simple as a stone, a flower or a feather, or it might be a parchment bearing writing; the meaning and significance that you attribute to the symbol is what is important. It can be created by yourself (to best effect) or by someone else, and works as a tool to activate our subconscious mind.

You can use general charms such as a cross, or a universally lucky symbol such as a horseshoe, but you will exude and therefore attract more potency and protection if you make and wear the appropriate charms with the matching gemstone, set in the right metal and created under the corresponding planetary influence. While most people wear silver or gold, cheaper tin or copper may be more appropriate and indeed beneficial for your Sun sign. An amulet (for protection) or a talisman or charm (for luck), must also be made, ordered, designed or purchased on the appropriate day of the week for its power to be most effective. Your day, as previously described, is Friday.

You can even go further and create or buy your amulet or charm at one of the hours and/or days when your planet is exerting its most powerful influence. It may sound complicated and requiring of forethought and effort, but if you are going to summon magic and are superstitious enough to truly *believe* that you can do this (and remember pure belief in something is the starting point of all manifestation), you should be scrupulous enough to do it properly. For your planet's day and time, please consult the information under the previous headings 'Your Lucky Day' and 'Venus's Magic Time Units'.

GODS, GODDESSES, ANIMAL TOTEMS & OTHER 'GUIDES'

Gods, goddesses and guides can be summoned to help you live your life to its optimal best. Some are connected with your Sun sign, while others may be of your own personal choosing, ones you may feel particularly drawn towards. Those which align with your ruling planet and your Sun sign, give a good indication of those who will shine a guiding light along your desired path, but you can choose your own too, based upon exploration, observations, research, meditation or simple intuition - I believe choosing your own, based on your inner *knowing* or guidance system, is a very powerful magical tool. However, to get you started, following are some animal spirit guide ideas for your contemplation. Good luck!

YOUR LUCKY ANIMALS & BIRDS

Hare, Dove, Owl, Songbirds, Swan, Sparrow, Cat, Hart, Lizard, Small Reptiles, Raven/Crow

"Somewhere beyond the walls of our awareness … the wilderness side, the hunter side, the seeking side of ourselves is waiting to return."
Laurens van der Post, *The Heart of the Hunter*

"(People) everywhere are being made acutely aware of the fact that something essentially to life and wellbeing is flickering very low in the human species and threatening to go out entirely. This 'something' has to do with such values as love, unselfishness, sincerity, loyalty to one's best friend, honesty, enthusiasm, humility, goodness, happiness … fun. Practically every animal has these assets in abundance and is eager to share them, given the opportunity and the encouragement."
Jay Allen Boone, *Kinship with All Life*

Some astrological systems, such as Shamanistic * or Native American Astrology, tell us that the Sun sign we were born under has a corresponding animal totem, which informs us about our characteristics and act as a kind of spiritual guide or mentor throughout our life's journey. These totems are described as Solar totems, because many of them share similarities with the Solar system and the sign the Sun was passing through at the time of our birth, and therefore relate to animals and animal behaviours which also correspond to environmental conditions and seasonal changes. These animals encompass many aspects of the Solar system, from seasonal relationships, to creature instincts, to reciprocal links with the planetary vibrations, and 'clans' within nature that you are inherently closely connected with through your date of birth.

Carl Jung, a master of dream analysis and interpretation, proposed that animals symbolise our natural instincts, operating through our dreams. He theorised that certain dream symbols, among them animals, represent core emotions and concepts, archetypes that will hold true for all of us the world over, regardless of so-called 'divisions' such as sex, customs, age or culture. In *Man and His Symbols*, Jung states that primitive societies believed that each person had a bush soul and a human soul. The bush soul incarnates as a tree or animal - a totem - and when the bush soul is harmed or injured, the human soul is considered injured as well.

Some of the most important and powerful spirit guides are those belonging to the animal kingdom. Both in ancient times and in some traditional modern tribal systems, people consult with animals for their wisdom and personal power. Even though most societies today have drifted away from this connection, it has never really left us, and different creatures continue to communicate with us on both the physical and spiritual planes in an attempt to speak to our souls and spirits.

As part of the teaching world, animals can bring us wisdom and survival skills, while others show us how to adapt, transcend or morph. Others still can remind us the importance of play and humour, and guide us around how to overcome life's challenges. Many are known for their loyalty and ability to love unconditionally and without judgement, while some have a grounded and healthy detachment, remaining true to themselves rather than pleasing others, an important lesson in itself. Whatever the qualities of the unique animal guides for your Sun sign, all have some enlightening soul-awakening traits that can teach us much about our own true inner selves. Ultimately, your animal spirit guides, and in particular your Solar totem animal, endow you with qualities that will enhance your life and help to activate your creativity, wisdom and intuition, helping to heal the broken or return the lost pieces of your soul and reconnect you to the natural world.

Your Solar totem animal (listed last on your lucky birds and animals list) is not the same as an animal spirit guide, which is based on metaphysical principles and is also based on your soul's mission in this embodiment - however, you can definitely make your birth Solar totem animal your spiritual guide if you wish, as you may find that its qualities, traits, symbolism and messages strongly reflect and define your own nature - or what you aspire to become, manifest or draw towards you. Your birth totem power animal comes from a place of trust and innocence, and represents the essence of your creative inner child. If you spend some time meditating on your Solar totem animal, asking what lessons it can teach, and reflect deeply on its character, life and habits, you may find it connects with you on a deep spiritual level and you can make the necessary changes to your life to draw in more magic and power.

Overall, if your life is stagnant or in need of healing or an energy boost, you can request your animal spirit or spirits to come and help you change your vibration, awaken your truth and arouse your inner forces. If you are aware of your animal spirit's presence in your life every day, you can use its particular energies to support, guide and teach you. And above all, pay attention to any signs and expressions of its lessons, and remember to thank your chosen animal guide for helping you.

* Shamanism is a traditional spiritual practice of the Native American culture. A shaman, one who practices this age-old art, is an intermediary between the human world and the world of the spirits. He inherits his magical powers at birth, but spends many years as an apprentice, so that he is usually much older in age before he is able to practice and call upon his skills. People ask for a shaman's help when there is a crisis on either a personal or wider spread scale, such as famine, drought, war or illness. The shaman makes contact with the spirits by going into a trance. First, he may perform a series of rituals, which usually include drumming, singing and chanting, and when these have brought on the right conditions, he leaves his body behind to travel to the other world. There he meets with the spirits of his ancestors, who inform him what must be done to relieve the suffering of his people. If the shaman is asked to cure someone of a dis-ease, then the spirits may accompany him to find the correct medicinal herbs or treatments for his patient.

YOUR FEATURE ANIMAL ★ RAVEN (OR CROW)

The Raven's Message ★ Bearer of magic, harbinger of messages from the cosmos
Brings the totem gift of ★ Easy going nature, flow, enthusiasm
Shares the power energies of ★ Entrepreneurship, well-received ideas, diplomacy, sociability
Brings forth and teaches the magic of ★ Romance, charm, balanced give and take in relationships

The Raven, or Crow, is the master magician, keeper of secrets and magic, and holder of the power of the unknown. With the Raven, something special is in the air, but we need to recognise it and ask ourselves how we can use it to spiritually grow. Often considered to be tricksters, Ravens are the guardians of sacred and esoteric mysteries. The Raven is blessed with keen eyesight, helping us to clearly see that which is before us. Ravens are associated with psychic powers and their feathers are sometimes used to aid clairvoyance. With this bird as your spiritual guide, you may well excel in the magical arts.

With high levels of enthusiasm and a natural entrepreneurial bent, the Raven is quite the charmer. Intelligent, clever and mystical, their charm flows effortlessly, easily and naturally. The Raven's smooth energy is well received by those around him, and everyone turns to the Crow for his opinions. This is because the Raven is both idealistic and diplomatic, and rather ingenious. Although the Raven can be demanding, vindictive, abrasive and inconsistent, in a nurturing and supportive environment, this Solar totem animal symbol is easy going, highly romantic, peace-loving and softly spoken. Further, the Raven can be quite patient, loving, giving and intuitive in relationships.

The Raven is the largest 'songbird' in North America, and is a highly intelligent and clever mimic. They can show us how to 'understand' animal language by their mimicry and use of the calls of other species in their own 'vocabulary'. They have even been known to learn and speak some human words.

Some early cultures feared the Raven and regarded them as bad omens, as they would feed on human corpses. In fact, the Raven's mythology and mysticism have a long history enshrouding them. Shamans know the power of a sudden piercing sound that accompanies shifting consciousness, and Ravens share this knowledge and power, giving out varied sounds, which can assist us in learning how to shift our own consciousness into various dimensional realms; this is why the Raven is regarded as a shape shifter with magical powers. Based upon this symbolism, people born under the Raven totem can expect many spiritual changes, epiphanies and awakenings throughout their lifetime.

Some Native tribes refer to the Raven as a keeper of secrets. They are believed to be linked to the 'void', a mysterious place in which Universal secrets are kept. Their black colour is linked to darkness, the place where unconscious fears can reside. In this way, Ravens are master magicians who represent transformational energy, assisting us to release our fears by delving into our inner selves and those dark places in order to illuminate them. The deepest healing can occur when we shine a light upon, confront and then resolve our inner conflicts.

If the Raven is your power animal, then magic and deep healing will abound in your life. The Raven's medicine can awaken these energies for you, especially those of conjury, connecting them to your will and intentions. With Raven as your special guide, you have the ability to make great changes, for the Raven knows the mysteries of life and is the guardian of the arcane, and is strongly linked with death and rebirth. It is important not to be afraid when this bird flies into your life, as he has great lessons to teach and wisdom to impart if you listen attentively and receive it mindfully. The Raven chooses its students according to their knowledge, and he will usually stay for as long as you need him, to help transmute karma and return you to the light. Further, he will lead you into your multidimensional self and reunite you with the inter-dimensional Universe.

The Raven is a powerful animal, whose wisdom includes introspection, self-knowledge, courage, healing, magic, creation, mysteries, shape shifting, mysticism, death, rebirth, and connection with other dimensions.

SPIRITUAL KEEPER ★ BEAR

Your spiritual keeper guides your spiritual growth and brings illumination. Your spiritual keeper is determined by the season in which you were born.

Regarded as the 'keepers' or 'caretakers' of the Universe, the four Directions or alignments were also referred to by the Native Americans as the Four Winds because their presence was *felt* rather than seen. The Direction to which your birth time belongs influences the nature of your inner senses. The West Direction's totem is the Bear. The Bear is a symbol of transformation, introspection, conservation, and strength drawn from within. The Bear has played a prominent role in many Native cultures, and because of its significance, a constellation, Ursus Major, was named for it. Bears can be amazingly fast and even climb trees, and many tribal people have regarded it as too powerful a medicine, fearing that the Bear would even hunt them and kill them if it was feeling threatened or starving. Despite its ferocity and the fear it can invoke, the Bear is considered to be a highly desired ally and spiritual keeper because of its fearless and instinctively protective powers. In many ways it is the epitome of the Great Protector, the protective mother. The Bear holds the teachings and wisdom of introspection.

Unlike other animals who are active during a specific time of day or night, the Bear is active *both* day and night, symbolising its connection with Solar energy, that of strength and power, and Lunar energy, that of intuition and the inner life. It enhances and teaches those born under this totem to develop both within themselves. Sometimes quick to anger and too sure of its own power, the Bear can throw caution to the wind and forget - to its detriment - that being unaware of its limits in certain situations can be disastrous. Bears, through their well-known hibernation periods during which they do not need to eat or drink for months at a time, teach us how to go within and find the resources necessary for our personal survival. People with Bear as their totem may find their own symbolic periods of Winter hibernation are opportune times to reflect, restore, and give birth to new ideas or projects which will take root and sprout in the springtime. This time of withdrawal or retreat represents the need to tap into our hidden strengths and teaches us to look inward in order to awaken the power of the subconscious in order to truly know oneself. Your animal keeper the Bear is, above all, a potent symbol of fearlessness, introspection and protectiveness.

CLAN ★ BUTTERFLY

Your clan animal comes from a place of inner knowing and intuition, helping you to discover the essence and magic of your true self. The Butterfly, a totem of the Air clan, represents and protects all that is beautiful and holds the secrets of change and personal transformation. The Butterfly symbolises that this transformation is always available to you, and may even begin without your conscious participation. Butterfly *is* the power of Air, the ability to float along on a breeze, and to 'dance' from place to place. They awaken our sense of lightness and joy, and teach us to dance with life rather than take it too seriously. In the folklore of some tribes, butterflies stand for change and balance, while in others ephemeral beauty, and some believe it to be symbolic of vanity and frivolity. Many tribes consider butterflies to be symbols of good luck, and some associate them with sleep and dreaming, decorating cradleboards and other children's items to help induce calm sleep and bring pleasant dreams. Butterflies symbolise metamorphosis, teaching us to trust in the process of change, re-awaken us to joy, and teach us that life is full of surprises and to therefore live with a constant sense of passion, intensity and wonder.

YOUR CORRESPONDING CHINESE ASTROLOGY ANIMAL

The Chinese Zodiac, known as Sheng Xiao (literally meaning 'birth likeness'), is based on a twelve-year cycle, each year in that cycle related to a particular animal. These animals are: Rat, Ox, Tiger, Rabbit, Dragon, Snake, Horse, Sheep, Monkey, Rooster, Dog and Pig. The selection and order of the animals that so influence people's lives, particularly in East Asian cultures, originated in the Han Dynasty (202 BC - 220 AD) and was based upon each animal's traits, characteristics, tendencies and living habits. Further, ancient people observed that there were twelve Full Moons in a year, and that, among other similarly related celestial observations, suggests its origins are also based on astronomical concepts.

The legend of the Chinese zodiac's story usually begins with the Jade Emperor, or Buddha (depending on who is telling the tale), summoning all the animals of the Universe for a race or a banquet. The twelve animals of the zodiac all appeared at the palace, and the order in which they arrived determined the order of the Chinese zodiac.

Each oriental animal corresponds with a Western astrology sign. For Libra, it is the Dog.

> "The martial strains have summoned me
> To hear your sorrows,
> Still your pain.
> I am the protector of Justice;
> Equality - my sole friend.
> My vision never blurred by cowardice,
> My soul never chained.
> Life without honour
> Is life in vain.
> *I am the Dog."*
> **Theodora Lau**

Chinese name for the Dog ★ GOU
Ranking Order ★ Eleventh
Hours ruled by the Dog ★ 7 p.m. to 9 p.m.
Direction ★ West - Northwest
Season and principle month ★ Autumn - October
Corresponds to the Western sign ★ Libra

★ **DOG** ★ *Fixed Element Metal*

★ Keywords ★

Loyal, honest, trustworthy, faithful, ethical, sharp-tongued, critical, selfish, stubborn, defensive, protective, noble, respectable, dutiful, intelligent

The Dog is the eleventh sign of the Chinese horoscope. Traditionally a yang animal, dogs are honest, devoted, attentive, modest and loyal. If they feel threatened, however, they can be guarded and defensive. Dogs are trustworthy and kind in their dealings with others but will react defensively if crossed. Your concern for the security and protection of yourself and your family can make you suspicious and critical, even self-righteous at times. You are willing to go to great lengths to support causes, even when everyone else has given up. Dog types are well-meaning, loving, helpful, firm and devoted friends with a great noble and moral flavour to their characters. You must, however, beware of people taking advantage of your desire to save the world, by looking after your own interests first and being a little less, well, dogged.

YOUR METALS

Libran power metals are Copper and Bronze.

Although the magic power of crystals is widely recognised and applied, the influence radiating from metals is often overlooked. Metal, too, emits a powerful energy and in fact, in Chinese philosophy, metal is considered so essential and powerful that it is classified as one of the elements, alongside Air, Fire, Earth and Water.

As already mentioned earlier in the book, throughout the writings of early philosophers and theorists, there are countless references to the unmistakable mystic connection between the seven known planets of the time, and Earthly affairs, ailments and objects. Seven metals were connected with the seven planets, to which seven colours and the seven 'transformations' were added. So the ancient alchemist came to share the astrological doctrine that each planet ruled a mineral: The Sun ruled gold, the Moon silver, Mars iron, Venus copper, Saturn lead, Jupiter tin, and Mercury quicksilver. Consequently, in alchemical symbolism the same sign came to represent the nominated metal and its corresponding planet.

COPPER

Copper is a chemical element with symbol Cu (from Latin *cuprum*), and carries a special cultural significance in that it was the first metal to be used by humans, its use believed to be as early as 7000 BC. Indeed, there is evidence it has been in use for at least 10,000 years. In alchemy, the symbol for copper was also the symbol for the goddess and planet Venus, your ruler. Aphrodite (Venus's Greek counterpart) and Venus represented copper in alchemy and mythology because of copper's lustrous beauty, its ancient use in producing mirrors, and its association with Cyprus, a place which had sacred links with the goddess.

Copper is a purely positive metal and when worn it is said to attract love (combining copper with emeralds makes a highly successful - and attractive - love amulet). Considered to hold sacred properties by various cultures in North America and India, copper is believed to stimulate healing and romance. Its healing reputation is well-known and widespread in the form of copper jewellery, worn to relieve certain physical ailments, and copper jewellery is also metaphysically used as a talisman to magnetise and maintain love, health, luck and prosperity.

Copper is prized by craftsmen for its elegance and lustre, and its ease of use in crafting things of great aesthetic appeal. For this, it is naturally considered a Venusian metal and so is associated with Taurus and Libra. Pure copper is reddish-orange/gold in colour and is soft and malleable, and like aluminium, it is 100 % recyclable without any loss of quality. As one of only two coloured metals, its attractiveness makes it highly desirable for making ornaments and jewellery.

Copper's main modern-day applications are its use in electrical implements and electrical wires (having very high thermal and electrical conductivity, and being ductile enough to be drawn into wire or beaten into sheets without fracturing), roofing and plumbing, industrial machinery, scientific instruments, and of course coins. The high resonance of copper makes it suitable for use in stringed musical instruments, such as violins, guitars and the double bass (traditional astrological thought associates the art of music with Venus). It is usually used as a pure metal, but when a greater hardness is required, it can be combined with other elements to make an alloy, such as brass or bronze. Copper's resistance to corrosion also makes it suitable for use in, or near the ocean. Brass, an alloy of zinc and copper, is used extensively in marine applications due to its non-corrosive nature.

Copper is even found in the human body in trace amounts and has various biological functions, mainly in the liver, muscle and bone.

Copper can also be made into jewellery, and it is believed that wearing a copper bracelet can relieve arthritis-related symptoms *^. It is also used in alternative medicine to various other ailments, as its absorption through the skin somehow creates a magnetic field, thereby affecting or treating nearby tissues ^.

Overall, copper serves many purposes and is arguably essential in keeping the world functioning, as it pervades in all facets of (comfortable) existence: it is found in your house, coin currency, transport systems, computers, cars, and cruise ships - all pretty essential things for the true Venusian experience, don't you think?

* However, in various studies, no difference has been found between arthritis treated with a copper bracelet, magnetic bracelet or placebo bracelet.

^ Please check with a medical professional before applying any remedy, treatment or concept outlined here

PLANTS, HERBS, SPICES, TREES, SHRUBS, FLOWERS, SCENTS & INCENSE

Plants have long been associated with magic, medicinal properties, superstition, nutrition and even astrology. In ancient times, some were endowed with magical properties based upon beliefs of the time, but also upon anecdotal evidence that some herbal concoctions, flowers or essences helped alleviate and even cure uncomfortable, painful or dis-eased physical or mental states. Whether these were based upon 'old wives' tales' or beliefs in supernatural forces matters little, for in modern times we can prove and indeed *have* proven through scientific research and controlled experiments, that plants have their place in our health and medicine cabinets. Some 'magical' plants have aphrodisiac or narcotic properties, while others have formidable toxic effects, but all are considered in some way to affect the human system on physical, spiritual and psychological levels. Plants such as cocoa, tobacco and coffee, which have accompanied humans over the course of millennia, are still, more than ever, an integral part of our daily lives. They still incite the same pleasures, the same fascinations, and the same dangers, and some still carry the same taboos. It is interesting to note that more than 80 per cent of chemical medicines in existence today, and found in pharmacists' dispensaries, are made from plants.

In modern astrology herbs are often associated with the zodiac signs and have evolved from an old system where a specific planet rules each herb. The planet that governs a herb is chosen according to its appearance, scent and where it grows; herbs are additionally categorised as hot or cold, and dry or moist. In this way you can see how the nature of the herb corresponds to the nature of the planet. If you are familiar with your ruling planets' basic associations, you will find it easy to match it to herbs. Although you can simply buy whatever herbs you wish to use for your magic, the optimum effect will be obtained if you can gather them at a favourable astrological time. Once you are armed with astrological knowledge, you can choose a time when the planet that rules your chosen herb is in a position of strength. Keep in mind that each planet rules a substantial amount of plants, so if one isn't easily obtained, it should be simply to find another one to use for the same purpose.

There sometimes seems to be a wide variance in the list of herbs associated with a specific astrological influence. This is because the different parts of the plant have different rulerships and uses. For example, whichever planet rules it, a plant that bears fruit is naturally related to Jupiter, its flowers relate to Venus, seed or bark to Mercury, leaves to the Moon, wood to Mars, and roots to Saturn. So, as well as the planet that traditionally rules the plant, it can be regarded as having a secondary ruler according to the part of the plant being used. Although you don't need to work with a highly complex system of deciding which herb will suit your purposes, you can make your magical workings more powerful by paying attention to some of these nuances.

Essentially, different scents, herbs, flowers and plants have their own specific vibrations. Their essences should be worn on your skin (you can make up your own combinations using essential oils or flower waters), burned in an oil burner, inhaled from a cloth, diffused in a bath or bowl of steam, or burned as incense sticks. Many plants, herbs and spices, however used, contain gentle yet effective energies which will affect not only your wishing ceremonies, but also your moods, associations and emotions, which can assist in carrying your wonderful Self in the direction of your dreams. Lifted up on incense smoke, for example, your wish is carried out to the wider Universe. Try making your own, out of any or all of your power plants, woods, flowers, shrubs, trees or herbs!

Thirty-three magical, mythical plants are: Cocoa, rosemary, tobacco, thyme, wheat, coffee, sugar cane, cinnamon, hemp, tea, pumpkin, foxglove, incense, amanita (a mushroom), tarragon, pepper, rice, belladonna, reed, ginseng, clove, ginger, sage, maize, mistletoe, lily, mandrake, St John's Wort, poppy, peyote, cinchona, verbena and the vine *. How many of your Libran 'lucky plants' (listed under the next sub-category, 'Your Lucky Plants, Herbs, Spices', etc.) can be found on this Magical 33 List?

YOUR LUCKY PLANTS, HERBS, SPICES, TREES, SHRUBS, FLOWERS, SCENTS, OILS & INCENSE

Rose, Daisy, Peach, Pear, Cleavers, Vanilla, Birch, Catmint, Silverweed, Ash, Fig, Almond, Walnut,

Violet, Poplar, Lilac, Cyclamen, Hydrangea, Juniper, Calendula, Primrose, White Sycamore, Pennyroyal, Feverfew, Yarrow, Forget-Me-Not, Thyme, Hydrangea, Burdock, Corn Silk, Parsley, Aloe, White Rose, Barley, Carnation, Cabbage Rose, Bearberry, Archangel, Uva Ursi, Dandelion, Buchu Leaves, Figwort, Prince's Pine, Vine, Mallow, Lemon Balm, Pansy, Mint, Cayenne, Thyme, Coriander, Fennel Seed, Dill, Angelica, Butcher's Broom, Violet, Dahlia, Garden Roses, Bluebell, all berry fruits, and all blue flowers. *

For Venus ★ Coriander, Valerian, Thyme, Myrtle. Venus is the planet of beauty, and the plants related to it contain fruits and a pleasant fragrance. Blackberry, Wild Cherry, Motherwort & Raspberry are all connected with Venus *

* Some plant products can be poisonous, toxic, hallucinogenic or even fatal if consumed. Always research first.

YOUR SPECIAL POWER FLOWERS

LIBRA IN GENERAL ★ Rose

OTHER BIRTH FLOWERS ★ Bluebell, Apple Blossom, Hydrangea & Love-In-A-Mist

SEPEMBER BORN ★ Aster ★ Grace, modesty and a sweetness of disposition are bestowed on those given the stylish aster, which is considered emblematic of elegance, friendship and secret love.

OCTOBER BORN ★ Calendula or Marigold ★ Those gifted with marigold, follower of the Sun, as their birth flower are spirited lovers of nature, radiating happiness to all around them. The marigold was associated with Apollo, the Greek god of the Sun. In Greek mythology, Nereid Clytie was spurned by Apollo and turned into a marigold - ever since then, marigolds have turned to face the Sun. The seeds of the marigold were often worn as an amulet to protect the wearer from theft, and they are frequently used in love charms and in wedding decorations. As a result, marigolds came to symbolise faithfulness and long-lasting unions.

YOUR FOODS

These sweet-toothed romantics with impeccable taste know their way around a pastry shop and view icing sugar as the stardust of the heavens. Sneak in a few savoury elements but keep them fragrant. Sociable, romantic, tasteful, artful and loving, the Libran is a bit of a connoisseur when it comes to food. In fact, a Libran probably invented the dinner party. You love most cuisines, as all types of foods appeal to you, however it must be of high quality and good standard, satisfying your need for impeccable presentation and good taste. Your ruling planet Venus rules the colour green, and earthy, leafy produce are a must in your kitchen. Loving of comfort and luxury, you enjoy dense, hearty, sustaining pleasures of the plate and palate - and no expense will be spared. You even make an art out of food, and can seemingly effortlessly produce delightful dishes. Aesthetically appealing food appeals to your senses, as does lavish presentation. You adore dining out in expensive restaurants, being waited on by your loved one, and equally love pampering others, as you make both a talented cook and a wonderful host - just don't be expected to do the dishes afterwards! Overall, the more well-presented, refined, classy and extravagant the dish, the more appealing you will find it! Hors douvres, canapés, oysters, caviar, vast platters, cheeses and French toast were made for the Libran palate. Fast, poorly presented, deep fried, sloppy and rushed are definitely not on the menu for the Scales.

LIBRA POWER FOODS

"Let food be your medicine; let medicine be your food."
Hippocrates

Perfumed, sweet-smelling and delicately flavoured foods all appeal to the Libran palate. Venison, Veal, Beef, Goat, Chicken, Partridge, Pheasant, Lobster, Sardines and Salmon are all flesh foods ruled by Venus. Artichokes, Sorrel, Asparagus, Parsnips, Corn, Almonds, Honey, Milk, Strawberries, Watercress, Spices, Apples, Currants, Beans, Oranges, Peaches, Celery, Apricots, Figs, Cherries, Grapes, Mangoes, Dates, Gooseberries, Raspberries, Spinach, Wheat Products of all Kinds and Confectionary are also your power foods. Your power beverages are Sherry, Fancy Cocktails, Port and Sweet Liqueurs. *

* Caution: Always use essential oils, alcohol and/or herbs with caution and research each one prior to use, as not all are safe for use by certain people, or under certain conditions such as pregnancy, intoxication or illness. Some herbs and oils may be hallucinogenic, toxic in high doses, or produce other undesirable effects, and may be considered potentially harmful or hazardous if used or consumed before operating machinery, driving, or combined with alcohol or other drugs. Always consult a qualified practitioner or undertake thorough research from reliable sources before use or consumption of any of the listed essential oils, herbs or foods.

YOUR LUCKY WOOD ★ SYCAMORE
(Great to make a magic wand out of!)

Native Americans referred to trees as 'Standing People' because they stand firm, obtaining strength from their connection with the Earth. They therefore teach us the importance of being grounded, while at the same time listening to, and reaching towards, our higher aspirations. In Norse mythology, Yggdrasil, the tree of life, is a cosmic map that represents all life. The tree has its roots in the Underworld, is linked to the Earth through its trunk and its branches reach into the air of the Otherworld of spirit. The dryad, or tree's spirit, needs to be respected and asked when 'taking' from a tree for the purposes of magic. The essence of tree magic lies in understanding the qualities of each type. These can be drawn on for such things as healing and spell-casting. For example, the rowan tree grows high up the sides of mountains, often in hard-to-reach places, so if you need to develop tenacity or access to difficult spiritual spaces, you can call on this tree; the oak tree is durable and strong, so if you are needing fortification or firmness, you can gain power from this tree. When respected as living, breathing beings, trees can provide insights into the workings of Nature, cycles, and our own inner essence. Each birth time is associated with a particular kind of tree, the basic qualities of which complement the nature of those born during that time. Appreciate the beauty of your affinity tree and study its nature carefully, for it has a connection with your own nature and lessons to impart.

SYCAMORE ★ Bestowing gifts of divination, prosperity, strength, love and harmony, sycamores are one of the oldest tree species on Earth. Symbolising growth, versatility, persistence and endurance, the sycamore is water-resistant and often grows where other trees cannot. In magic, it is useful for askings involving growth, and having regenerative properties, can be used for restorative purposes. Sycamore symbolises development, vitality and perseverance and is good to use for any magic involving prosperity, love and longevity. Believed to bring success and abundance, it can also teach humility.

YOUR SACRED CELTIC CALENDAR TREES ★ VINE (MOON) OR IVY (MOON)

VINE MOON ★ (2 September - 29 September)
IVY MOON ★ (30 September - 27 October)

The Celts and other ancient peoples had many beliefs and traditions based around the magical lore of trees. The system of Celtic tree astrology was developed out of a natural connection with the Druids' knowledge of Earth cycles and their reverence for the sacred knowledge they believed was held by trees. The Druids had a profound connection with trees and regarded them as vessels of infinite wisdom. Their calendar, being based on a Lunar year of thirteen months, contains a tree for each of these

Lunar months, corresponding with (but not exactly) each of the twelve western astrology zodiac signs, which are based on the Solar calendar. Because there are some crossovers, I have included two possible trees for your zodiacal birth period.

VINE MOON ★ Three of the 13 Celtic Moon months are governed by plants other than trees. Your birthday, if it falls between 2 September and 29 September, is ruled by the Vine Moon, which is a time to harvest the rewards of all your efforts through the year so far. Vine brings strength, durability and prosperity, and is associated with the fruition of plans as well as symbolising 'bacchanalian' pleasures and joy. In Celtic astrology, the vine is often linked with grapes, although this fruit is not native to the British Isles. Because of this, it is thought that the Druids used the native blackberry or bramble vines in their symbolic mythology instead, connecting the twining of vine plants to their beliefs in the spiralling growth of life energy. Both plants represent forces of vitality and life; and like the grapevine, bramble vines are associated with joy, livelihood, wellbeing and exhilaration, both types providing wine and food. Certainly in colder European climates, the grapevine was reluctant to grow, and its place was taken, spiritually and practically, by the bramble or blackberry; therefore, it is thought by Celtic scholars that the Druids used the blackberry vine rather than the grape one for their Celtic Moon month calendar. The Vine Moon occurs at the Autumnal Equinox and is a time of harmony when days and nights are of equal length, symbolising balance. The Vine Moon is traditionally a time for plans to move into a period of fruition or harvest before the (northern hemisphere) winter sets in. It represents a time of plenty when life's cup is full and the fruits of labour are to be enjoyed.

Vine types, being born within the Autumnal Equinox, are considered to be changeable, indecisive, full of contradictions and unpredictable. It is hard for you to 'pick sides', as you can see all angles equally and can empathise with each. There are aspects of life about which you are really sure, however, and these include good food, wine, art and music. A connoisseur of refinement and quality, you sit easily with luxury and have the Midas touch when it comes to transforming drab into beautiful. Classy, charming and elegant, you win others over with your classic style and poise. Although at times unpredictable, this usually just adds to your mystique.

IVY MOON ★ Three of the 13 Celtic Moon months are governed by plants other than trees. Your birthday, if it falls between 30 September and 27 October, is ruled by the Ivy Moon, which is an opportune time to cast a little magic to boost your health. A spiralling symbol of immortality and magic, the ivy provides the key to the Otherworlds and the kingdom of the fairies. In the Celtic lore, fairy folk, the Sidhe, were said to have once walked the Earth in the realm of mortals. Since their retreat to the fairy kingdom in the Otherworld, they are now only seen as butterflies. This insect was assigned to the ivy by the Druids, because the spiralling plant was thought to open an entrance to the world of the Sidhe. The short lifespan of the butterfly (about one month) also associates this elegant creature - and fairies - with the phases of the Moon.

Ironically, although ivy was chosen as a ruler of one of the Celtic Moon months, this plant actually destroys the health of trees by growing all over them, effectively choking them, and stealing their nourishment from surrounding soil. In effect, it is a parasite that clings to trees and walls by tiny 'adhesive' roots that grow out from its stem, and its tenacious nature means that it is difficult to eradicate or discourage. It is a persistent, hardy and long-lived evergreen plant that can adapt to a huge range of environments. Due to its strength and longevity, it has become associated with the enduring immortality of the spirit. Growing in a spiral formation towards the sky, it can be found just as easily on derelict buildings and dying trees - it is indeed a symbol of resurrection.

Ivy types are most noted for their sharp intellects and their ability to overcome all odds. Compassionate and loyal, you have a giving nature, but being born during the time of a waning Sun, you can encounter more challenges in life than most. You do, however, endure these troubling times with a soulful grace and silent perseverance. Although you are softly spoken, you have a keen wit, charm and charisma that holds you in good stead in social settings.

ESPECIALLY FOR AUSTRALIANS
(OF ALL ZODIAC SIGNS)

If you live in Australia, here are two Australian-based magical woods, for those who prefer to source their woods closer to home and nature. Australia has a less documented history than many European civilisations, but still has no less mythology and legends swirling in its mists of time.

EUCALYPTUS ★ Eucalyptus is very plentiful and has a wonderfully intoxicating, distinctive, clean aroma which is reminiscent of the continent's vast areas of bushland, and has played an important ceremonial and medicinal role in the culture of Australian Aborigines, who have inhabited the nation for 40,000 to 50,000 years. Eucalyptus is a wood of feminine energy whose elemental association is Earth and main origin is Australia. One of the strongest healing woods known, eucalyptus wood has been used for centuries for medicinal as well as ritualistic purposes. Heady and Earthy, the energy of this wood is clean and pure. Eucalyptus is recommended for the promotion of good, robust health, and is also related to luck, especially if regarding knowledge. An excellent tool in divination, particularly when worn as a charm to invoke luck, it brings the wearer or user good fortune when used in rituals seeking positive results.

LEOPARDWOOD (or LACEWOOD) ★ Leopardwood or the Leopard Tree, so named because of its spotted wood, carries the energies of both the masculine and the feminine, Mars (Aries, Scorpio) and Venus (Taurus, Libra), and its main affinity is with the Water element (Cancer, Scorpio, Pisces). Leopardwood is a very useful tool for divination and is associated with positive luck, earning it the label 'gambler's wood'. Overall, its energy is very positive, making it an ideal wood for use in almost any ritual or spell, especially those concerning luck, magic and divination.

THE POWER OF LOVE

Each Sun sign exudes their own love and romance style. This style is an energy unique to that sign, and has the power to magnetise to that person their true, soulful match. Unhappy or unsuccessful relationships are often the result of incompatible Sun signs, personal values, goals, hopes, viewpoints or expectations. I believe everyone has a perfect soul partner (or three!) who is especially for them, and just knowing that special person or persons are out there can illuminate your life's romantic path. In this lifetime, we may not find that person or persons, but can still experience the joys and wonders of many other significant relationships which enrich and add tremendous meaning to our lives. Some partnerships are only fleeting, but the feelings they give us can last a lifetime, while others are more enduring, and the rewards they give us and lessons they teach us can last a lifetime too. Small gestures of love on a frequent basis, consistent nurturing and communication, and making the effort to understand each other, are just four ways to keep the fires of passion and romance burning long after the initially roaring fire has diminished into glowing embers.

Your whole natal chart would need to be examined to form an overall picture of your romantic nature, and although the Sun is a fantastic starting point, it is not the sole consideration. Regarding these other planets, in Carl Jung's studies on psychological astrology, and in traditional synastry (the comparing of two people's natal charts to determine overall compatibility), the harmonious link between the Sun in one person's chart and the Moon in the other's (usually the man's Sun and the woman's Moon) is considered the best indication for a happy and enduring relationship. More specifically, the sextile aspect, an angle of 60 degrees, appeared most frequently between the Sun of one and the Moon of the other in fulfilling relationships. Other positive planetary contacts, such as one person's Moon to another's Venus, or the Mars to the Moon (again, traditional indications of attraction and harmony) also occurred frequently.

The feminine personal planets in a male's chart (Moon and Venus), and the masculine personal planets in a female's chart (Sun and Mars) tell a lot about the inner self and how this is projected onto relationships. However helpful chart analysis is in telling a story about your relationship style and approach, it all depends not on your chart, but on what you do with the resources at your disposal, which your chart can indeed tell you a lot about. Relationships and marriages involving harmonious planetary and zodiacal energies between the two people tend to last longer because they are simply more 'flowing' and easier.

The signs in which the four personal and 'relationship' planets - the Sun, the Moon, Venus and Mars - are placed, coupled with the aspects they make with the other planets in the chart, give important clues into understanding the often unconscious drives within you that shape your relating style, tastes, mannerisms and patterns.

Expanding upon the other planetary considerations is beyond the scope of this book, but it is useful to know, particularly if you are interested in examining the dynamics of a current relationship a bit deeper, or are wishing to attract a new one into your life. But for now, your Sun sign is a wonderful place to start! Your Solar sign is regarded as being at the core of the complex - and very fun - study of relationships! So for now, we will begin this study of love with your essence, your core self, the brightest light shining from within - your Sun sign!

SOME LUCKY-IN-LOVE TIPS
GENERAL HINTS

★ To attract and retain love, the Heart chakra (an energy centre within the body) needs to be balanced and clear from blockages. The Heart chakra is located in the region of the physical heart. Its Sanskrit name is *anahata*, and its symbol is a twelve-petal green lotus flower whose centre contains a green circle and two intersecting triangles making up a six-pointed star representing balance (and also could be said to symbolise six as the number of Venus). Its element is Air and its colour is green. Balance in this chakra is expressed as unconditional love for ourselves and others. Crystals that can be used to cleanse and balance this chakra are mostly green and pink stones.

★ Pink candles (two, representing a couple, or six, representing Venus, is preferable) can be used in love spells.

★ Any 'love-attracting' wishing rituals should be done on a Friday (ruled by Venus) night around the time of the New Moon (signifying the principle of increase and growth).

★ Basil, otherwise known as witch's herb or St Joseph's wort, is said to be the most potent lover herb of all. Basil vibrates to the energy of Mars, which is all about lust and sexual energy, and it is used prolifically in all sorts of love potions and rituals throughout the world.

★ Ginger has a reputation as a potent sexual tonic and aphrodisiac *. Arousing and warm, it can increase sensual vitality, particularly in men. Being warming and spicy, its vibration aligns with Mars. Saffron is also regarded as a potent, albeit expensive, aphrodisiac!

★ Wear red and pink (associated with Mars and Venus respectively), as these colours in all their shades are said to incite passion, lust and romance. Green is also connected with the heart by virtue of its association with the Heart chakra and the planet Venus, and its links with fertility, nature, abundance of all kinds, and new growth.

★ Call upon some higher spiritual help. When working your 'love magic', some planetary influences, goddesses and gods that you can call upon are: Aphrodite, Venus and Eros/Cupid, and other lesser known deities such as Juno Lucina, Demeter, Freya, Ishtar, Circe and Hathor.

★ The planet Venus has developed a rich culture of gods and goddesses associated with her varying levels of love and passion. These include the virgin - Brighid; the fertile woman - Aphrodite, (the Greek goddess); and of course Venus (the Roman equivalent); the mother and provider - Demeter; and desirous or physical love - Eros/Cupid (Venus's son).

★ The pine tree is sacred to Adonis (Venus's lover) and is said to balance the male and female energies. Pine is cleansing and protective and, as an evergreen, symbolises life. Its cones represent fertility.

★ Cardamom is said to have aphrodisiac qualities ★ The three almost universally recognised symbols of love are the goddesses Venus and Aphrodite, and the Cupid. Venus is the patroness of flowers and vegetation, and represents the regenerative cycle of creation, as well as beauty, herbs and physical love. She can be called upon for general love wishes and rituals. The dove, roses, rings, copper, apples, rosemary and the ankh are some of her sacred symbols. Aphrodite is a Greek goddess who has the ability to brings lovers together. Her names mean 'of the sea' as she is believed to have been born of the foam of the ocean. She can be called upon in ceremonies and spells for affection, love, marriage and partnership. Some of her associated symbols are the Flower of Aphrodite, swans, dolphins, frankincense and myrrh. Cupid, the cherubic winged boy with a bow and arrow, is the Roman name, and Eros is the Greek name for the same deity. The son of Venus/Aphrodite, he is an aspect that represents lustful love and desire.

★ Heartsease, another name for the wild pansy, Latin viola tricolour, was one of the most popular additives to the love potions of the ancient Romans and Greeks.

★ In centuries past, when people were more in tune with nature and its cycles, ceremonies, rituals and festivals were held on certain dates or times of year. The following are some examples, and you can reawaken their powers through craft and ceremony: February 2 is Bridhid's Day, or Bride's Day, and represents the white goddess; February 14 is Valentine's Day, traditionally the greatest and most well-known love 'celebration' of the year; March 1 is one of the festival days of Juno Lucina, the light bearer and goddess of women and marriage; the month of April is especially linked to the love goddess Aphrodite; the Summer solstice which falls on or around June 21 is an important time for reconnecting with the spirit of love, fertility and marriage; August 1 is the first of three harvest festivals in the Celtic calendar: The Harvest Festival honours Demeter, the goddess of love, as bountiful mother and faithful wife; the Festival of Lights, Diwali, in October, is sacred to Lakshmi, the Hindu goddess of happiness, love, and good fortune; the Winter solstice which falls on or around December 21, marks the turning point from long dark nights to lengthening days, and is the time of the wheel of love when virgin goddesses gave birth to their children - it is also fittingly symbolised by evergreens such as pine, ivy and holly; in Mexico, December 31, the last night of the year, is traditionally 'wishing night' and is an opportune time to make a wish for a lover in the coming year, using evergreen branches to enhance your request.

* The term 'aphrodisiac' is derived from Aphrodite, the Greek goddess of love, beauty, lust and sensuality

★ GEMSTONES ★

When it comes to calling love into your life using crystals, the general rule is that any of the pink or green stones are closely aligned with matters of the heart and can therefore help you to entice the affections you seek. Although your Sun sign has its very own special gemstones, outlined elsewhere in the book, the following stones can be used by all the signs (except for the first point, which are your own sign's feature stones), as their energies and qualities contain the power to attract and create love in all its forms, from self-love to deeper soulful connections with another, or to increase states of being which open the heart, thus enhancing your abilities to magnetise love.

★ Opal, Tourmaline and Sapphire ★ Using your Libran luckiest crystals is a fabulous start to working on heightening your romantic zest, and making your sensual energy more potent. Jade, Rose Quartz, and Diamond are also useful in raising your attracting powers.

★ Rose Quartz is the ultimate love stone. It invites love into your life by helping to open your heart to receive love, and gently reminding you that you are worthy of love. Connected with the Heart chakra, it is the stone of unconditional love, enhancing all forms of it and opening up the heart. It is excellent for increasing self-worth and acceptance. The colour of rose quartz is pink, the colour of Venus, the amorous planet of desire and nurturance. Balancing and calming, it helps to heal emotional pain. Wear this stone, keep some beside your bed, or sleep with some under your pillow to remind you that love it coming your way - and that you whole*heart*edly deserve it!

★ Green Aventurine is considered the 'opportunity and luck stone'. Connected with the Heart chakra, it helps us to recognise opportunities and is said to place us exactly where we need to be for good things to transpire, as energetically it opens our mind and heart to increased perception to recognise lucky elements. It also promotes new growth, optimism, and is an overall attractor of good fortune, adventure and abundance.

★ Jade, on a spiritual level, has an affinity with the Heart chakra. It harmonises relationships, and encourages compassion and the establishment of strong bonds.

★ Emerald is reputedly a stone of constancy in love, and is said to have been brought to Earth from the planet Venus. Because it is green, it also holds deep associations with the Heart chakra.

★ Rhodochrosite can be used to attract one's soul mate. This stone, as with all the pink stones, can be used as an effective love magnet. It encourages you to appreciate yourself by teaching you that you are worthy of love, wholeness and happiness - and so opening you up to receive.

★ Malachite, Citrine, Rhodonite, Moonstone, Morganite, Beryl, Ruby, Mangano Calcite, Garnet, Red and Pink Tourmaline, Tugtupite, Rutilated Quartz, Lodestone, Peridot and Lapis Lazuli are also known for their love properties, and can be used or worn to invite romance into your life, or to bring and retain enduring love.

★ Clear Quartz can be used with any of these listed crystals to amplify their metaphysical properties.

★ Shells: Although shells are not technically a crystal, but rather a natural elemental material, they are associated with love and are sacred to Aphrodite, the Greek love goddess, and are often used in magic talismans to attract romance.

★ ESSENTIAL OILS ★

The following essential oils are known for their aphrodisiac or love-attracting properties also, and can be worn as perfumes on the skin, used in an oil burner or vaporiser, dispersed in a bath, used in spell-casting and wishing rituals, sprinkled on your pillow to imbue your dreams with inspired romantic notions, or in any other creative ways you can think of! **

★ Essential oils, flowers and herbs which contain natural pheromones or like substances, or increase pheromone levels in the body, are: Lavender, Frankincense, Jasmine, Nutmeg, Ylang Ylang, Sandalwood, Patchouli and Asian Agarwood (Oud).

★ The prime love oil, which holds Universal appeal, is rose. Reputedly excellent for both the mind and body, roses are the basis of more than 95 per cent of women's fragrances, and the petals have a long tradition of uplifting the spirits and soothing the soul. *Rosa damascena* is believed to be good for attracting love, while *R. centifolia*, the French rose oil base, is regarded as an aphrodisiac. Rose is traditionally accepted as the all-encompassing Universal fragrance of love, blessed with a reputation for opening up the hearts of all those who come under its spell.

★ Cedarwood oil has been used since ancient times in incense and perfumes. Its deep, woody scent helps to stimulate the Base chakra, increasing sexual passion and desire. Its sedative qualities aid relaxation and encourage openness. In herbal magic, it is also associated with spells for wealth and abundance.

★ Neroli, Geranium, Almond (as a base), Basil, Thyme, Vetiver, Gardenia, Vanilla, Rose Otto, Apple, Cardamom, Lotus, Orange, Ginger, Bergamot, Rosewood and Clary Sage are also exquisitely seductive and sensual, and can be used in any way you like to bring to you that which your heart desires. These oils, when mixed with your own pheromones and magical intentions, will naturally enhance your point of attraction!

** Always research first and use with caution.

LIBRA ★ LOVE STYLE

Love to Libra is like breathing is to life. To Libra love is open, harmonious and friendly, and you come across as glamorously ethereal. As a lover and in relationships, you adore being in love and are accommodating and compromising. Ruled by the planet of love, you have a gift for the art of living, and for the art of loving. Charming, cultured, stylish and seductive, you glide through life with the effortless grace of a butterfly, picking up many admirers along the way. This is no surprise, given that you're the zodiac's biggest flirt. Since you strive for a harmonic and peaceful coexistence with another, you use your diplomacy and tact to get along wonderfully with all other signs. Your biggest snag may be the fact that you are so indecisive - one can sometimes wait a long time for Libra to offer a genuine emotional response which hasn't been reflected over, for days preceding it, and it may also take you a long time to settle down, or, being so easily swept away by romance, you may settle down with Mr or Mrs Wrong and realise it too late. For this reason, many Librans will probably encounter at least one divorce in their lifetime. Plus, you are the sign of marriage, so you are bound to be a sucker for nuptials and the glitz and glamour of a wedding and honeymoon. Fidelity may also be an issue for you, as you love to circulate among as many people as possible and often, particularly in your younger years, find it hard to be 'tied down' in an exclusive relationship. This is due to your Airy nature, which lends you an air of detachment and need for social connection.

Overall, you are capable of putting an enormous amount of energy and effort into your relationships, and your need for harmony and balance so pronounced, that you may compromise to a fault. But in any case, Libra is the master of relationships and intuitively knows a lot about them, not through experience necessarily but through an inborn, natural knowing - and your partner is usually the lucky beneficiary of your skill. You may occasionally just need to be reminded that discussing love is not the same thing as demonstrating it, feeling it, showing it, emoting it; you are, after all, an Air sign who resides primarily in the mind. Hiding behind captivatingly aloof façade, however intriguing, will only take you so far in matters of the heart.

LUCKY IN LOVE? LIBRA ★ COMPATIBILITY

* Please note the following is based on your Sun sign alone. For a whole and integrated approach to relationship compatibility, your whole natal chart would need to be taken into consideration. Synastry (*syn*: acting or considered together, united; *astry*: pertaining to the stars) is a branch of astrology which delves into more complex areas, and is based upon the natal charts of the two people concerned, to determine overall compatibility, potential conflicts and suitability based upon celestial influences. For the purposes of length, the below information is simplified and only refers to Sun sign connections.

Libra ★ Aries ♎ ♈

The loud and tactless Ram can upset Libra's delicate sensibilities. As Libra's natural opposite, Aries also wields a pull-push attraction, one moment irresistible, the next impossible. Opposites attract so you two are good friends and lovers. The Ram just shouldn't take Libra's seductive charm too seriously - it's often just a harmless game for them. Fire works well with Air, and you two have the potential to share an intense and explosive meeting of the spirits. Since these two signs are naturally friendly and need the company of others, they can share these pleasures together. However, Libra is the epitome of the personal lover, while Aries is the archetypal selfish 'me-first' lover, whose needs are paramount in the relationship. Libra's constant weighing and vacillating may irritate the Aries, and his indecisiveness may attract or repel.

If a conflict arises between you, you will stay and fight while Libra gets upset or leaves. Initially, there is often a strong attraction between you, and once it slows down to a smouldering simmer, the diplomatic Scales will usually be able to smooth any ruffled Arien feathers, making the relationship work. While Aries is largely spontaneous, blunt and frank, acting now and thinking later, Libra uses diplomacy, grace and tact to handle things. Neither will make impossible demands on the other, as both are intellectually-based rather than feeling, smothering types, but this relationship can only work if Libra allows Aries the independence he seeks and does not demand too much of him, for the Ram is childlike and as free as the wind by nature, and needs room to explore and adventure.

Overall compatibility rating ★ 8.5 out of 10
Lucky Romance Tip ★ To attract an Aries, wear the colours red or orange, and use the crystal diamond

Libra ★ Taurus ♎ ♉

Mutually ruled by the lovely Venus, you both represent different aspects of this planet. The slow Taurean may seem conservative and too strait-laced for the Libran's ethereally romantic spirit. Since you are both ruled by the famed planet of love, you should have a lot in common - however, Earth and Air don't blend easily, and Libra is guided by the intellect while Taurus is led by its senses. But Taurus will be no doubt be intrigued and captivated by the graceful, easy going and charming Scales, and his chivalrous nature will win the Bull's heart. Both of you are warm, affectionate, sensuous and aesthetically aware by nature, and share a love of the arts, beauty and luxurious things. Taurus could be a little materialistic for the more ethereal and idealistic Libra, and being an Air sign, Libra will not tolerate being possessed by the clingy Bull. Security is the last thing on the Scales' mind, as they would prefer to share a deep mental affinity in their relationships, and see love as one of the many pleasures in life to be enjoyed without great attachment. Taurus will also not appreciate the naturally flirty Libra's wandering eye either, and will become jealous and brooding if she suspects Libra of being unfaithful. Being a Cardinal Air sign, the Scales will resent any restrictions to their freedom of movement, especially in social circles, in which they thrive. The Bull would rather dwell in the comfort of her home while Libra would much prefer to be on the social circuit; this major difference between you could give rise to substantial conflict. Overall, your mutual ruling planet Venus may well provide the bond that can glue you together, and because harmony and peace are vitally important to both of you, neither one is likely to provoke discord in the relationship. Although Taurus is stubborn, Libra can tactfully and cleverly manipulate the Bull's obstinacy into submission without the Bull even knowing it. Also, Libra is the sign of marriage and partnership, so this could link in well with Taurus's urge for relational security - or if your love breaks down, you could still make fine business partners, as you both have an innate sense for business and enterprise.

Overall compatibility rating ★ 7.5 out of 10
Lucky Romance Tip ★ To attract a Taurus, wear the colours pink or green, and use the crystal rose quartz

Libra ★ Gemini ♎ ♊

Two Air signs tango very nicely, yet Gemini remains an enigma to the Scales. Libra admires the Twins' mental agility yet may find him a little exhausting. Geminian liveliness will boost Libran energy levels, and the placid Libran influence will undoubtedly calm the Twins' restlessness. However, Gemini may not be able to provide the security that Libra is seeking. Two Air signs, both oozing natural charm, make for a fine friendship, but if Gemini would like to be more than friends with the Scales, he will need to curb his talking and listen more. Air harmonises with Air, and these two have the potential to have a delightful and stimulating meeting of the minds. This combination also blends Mercury, the planet of the mind, with Venus, the planet of love, creating a mutual appreciation between you of all that is sociable, beautiful, artistic, refined, interesting and spirited. The two of you together mix intellect, charm and esprit, and you are both flirtatious, so a strong mutual attraction will be likely as soon as you meet. Since these two signs are naturally friendly and need the company of others, they can share these pleasures together. However, Libra's emphasis on close intimate relationships may cause tensions, as Gemini needs to feel free, unencumbered and able to indulge in many adventures and activities. While Gemini talks now and thinks later, Libra uses diplomacy, grace and tact to handle things. Neither will make impossible demands on the other, as both are intellectually-based rather than feeling, smothering types, but this relationship can only work if Libra allows Gemini the freedom to explore and does not demand too much of the Twins. Your intellectual rapport alone however, suggests deep potential here, and can take your relationship to great heights. And one thing is certain, boredom will most certainly never be a feature.

Overall compatibility rating ★ 9 out of 10
Lucky Romance Tip ★ To attract a Gemini, wear the colours light blue or yellow, and use the crystal citrine

Libra ★ Cancer ♎ ♋

This challenging combination of Libra's Air and Cancer's Water can seem a bit staid for the rather detached, Airy Libran. When the Crab tries to cling onto Libra with her firm pincers, Libra will tend to wriggle free with all his might. However, although Water and Air are generally not very compatible, your rulers the Moon and Venus vibrate to a harmonious energy and give this relationship a warm, cosy feeling. Both peace-loving, affectionate and giving, there is good potential here. Cancer is easily hurt but unless Libra is provoked he is unlikely to do or say anything to cause any conflict in the union. If trouble does arise, both of you would sooner scuttle off than confront the other, but both in your different ways of course - Libra's way is denial, avoidance and evasiveness, Cancer's simply to hide away until the storm passes. Also, the normally balanced Libran would never do anything to upset the Scales or cause the relationship to get out of kilter. Cancer's natural desire to love and protect will be appreciated by Libra, however if it spills over into clinginess the Airy, rather more detached Scales will feel put out. Another point of difference is that Libra is intellectually-based and Cancer is emotions-based, which could cause rifts, as Libra strikes a fine balance between reason and emotion, so may be unsettled by Cancer's excess of feelings. The Crab's childish sulking will also not be tolerated by the more sophisticated Libran, and Cancer will want deeper levels than the more superficial Libra is willing to open up to her. Libra also pays too much attention to outward appearances, which could dishearten Cancer. Overall though, you are both romantic and loving, so if you can build a bridge over any differences and get over them, this could be a heavenly and enchanting pairing.

Overall compatibility rating ★ 7.5 out of 10
Lucky Romance Tip ★ To attract a Cancerian, wear the colours silver or white, and use the crystal moonstone

Libra ★ Leo ♎ ♌

The roaring Lion can be hugely attractive to the impressionable Libran, yet if the Fire dwindles your relationship rapidly wears thin. Libra's fence-sitting may irritate the more decisive, determined Leo.

Libra's charm and grace soothes the Lion's Fiery soul, yet the Scales' indefinite, fluctuating rhythms can frustrate Leo's need for action, drama and excitement. But Fire is compatible with Air and since both of you have the natural ability for enjoying all the good things in life, there is no doubt many happy times will be had together. In any case, you are both charming, sociable, friendly and loving. Libra has an ethereal, measured approach to those good things in life however, and the Lion's extravagance, lavishness, generosity and flamboyance may well upset the Libran's fine need for balance and peace. Despite this, the Lion will be most impressed by the Libran's impeccable manners, style and good (and expensive) tastes, and the Scales will appreciate the Leo's chivalry, warmth and even vanity. A curious feature in your partnership is that although Leo likes to be boss, Libra is an efficiently cool customer and will be able to tactfully and artfully manipulate the Lion - and the Lion will never know it. Libra is much more diplomatic than Leo, who likes to get his own way, but this difference does not necessarily make for a clash of wills. Overall, you are likely to get along just fine and make a successful and happy partnership through developing a fun-loving, light-hearted rapport. The Lion just needs to tone down his loud roar to suit the Libran's innate need for balance and harmony, and romantic bliss can indeed be yours.

Overall compatibility rating ★ 8.5 out of 10
Lucky Romance Tip ★ To attract a Leo, wear the colours gold or orange, and use the crystal ruby

Libra ★ Virgo ♎ ♍

If Virgo picks holes in Libra or tries to organise him 'into shape', the Scales will drift away on the next fanciful whim, looking elsewhere for stimulation and mental rapport. Libran charm can seem a little wishy-washy to the Virgin, and their indecision can drive the Virgo mad, yet Virgo is also enchanted by Libra's easy grace, natural warmth, wit and sociability. Libra may make demands that seem superfluous to the modest and sensible Virgin, but for talents in mastering life, relationships and love, Virgo can certainly learn something here. The marked contrast usually present in Earth/Air combinations is not so apparent here, as you are both mind-based and not overtly emotional, so won't make excessive demands on the other. You complement each other in many ways and both like to achieve some degree of perfection. Further, you both have a good sense of style, sensuality and discerning tastes. Because Libra seeks, above all else, to achieve harmony, balance, beauty and to keep the peace, he is unlikely to provoke the normally critical, fault-finding Virgo. But socialite Libra may be rather too flighty for the steady Virgo, who strives for consistency and stability, and Libra is dependent on his social contacts whereas

Virgo only trusts her own efforts. If Virgo becomes nit-picky of Libra's faults, the Libra will not hesitate to find new company. But overall, this is a graceful, understated union, with both of you being gentle, caring, courteous and considerate of the other at all times.

Overall compatibility rating ★ 7 out of 10
Lucky Romance Tip ★ To attract a Virgo, wear the colours white or yellow, and use the crystal sapphire

Libra ★ Libra ♎ ♎

When two Librans join forces, mental affinity and sexual chemistry produce a double dose of charm, wit, long discussions and romance. Here the charmer falls for his own tricks. Although this union has all the pointers leaning toward being a harmonious one, a lack of decision-making power and over-indulgence in life's pleasures could prove hindrances to both your mental resources - *and* your purse-strings! There is little conflict when Air mixes with Air, and since you are both ruled by Venus, the planet of love, balance, art and beauty, it will be easy to agree on most things. Any type of conflict or discord will upset you both, and so you try to avoid these at all costs and keep the relationship on an even keel - which you both seem to do artfully and effortlessly. You are both graceful, gentle, gregarious and easy going and make a wonderfully sociable, affable duo on the social scene. However, all this blissed-out harmony may mean your union lacks the fighting spirit, so this is not the most progressive team. Your home-life and lifestyles will certainly reflect the elegance and aesthetics which is so important to the Scales. Overall, this is a delightful match and meeting of the minds, but sooner or later decisions need to be made and action needs to be taken to stop this relationship becoming stagnant. Indeed, there is a profound empathy between the two of you, but the big question is whether or not you will ever actually achieve anything of great value or betterment.

Overall compatibility rating ★ 8 out of 10
Lucky Romance Tip ★ To attract another Libran, wear the colours pink and blue, and use the crystal opal

Libra ★ Scorpio ♎ ♏

Scorpio can see through the Libran's games and know when they are serious or just flirting. Scorpio enjoys the challenge and the magnetism the Scales so effortlessly provide but will not forgive infidelity or sharing the Scales with anyone else. Even though you two operate on different wavelengths, Libra is drawn to Scorpio's intelligent insights. Libra may even surprise himself by appreciating the brooding seriousness of this passionate sign. This is an intriguing combination and surprisingly it often works. Libra goes to enormous lengths to get along with everyone, whereas Scorpio just exudes a magnetic appeal which attracts many. As the Scales seek balance in all areas of their life, especially relationships, the Scorpio will provide him with this stability, and you will both equally dedicate yourself to making the partnership work if you feel it is worthwhile. However, the long-term prospects may be doubtful - Scorpio's complexity may unsettle the harmony-seeking Scales, who never likes to be tipped too far in any one direction. If this union is to work, Scorpio will need to rein in her excessive need to control and possess, and cultivate greater refinement to suit the Libran. Scorpio thrives on living life to the extreme, and her all-or-nothing attitude may fluster the normally unflappable Libran. However, your elements Air and Water may also combine well, because your rulers, the feminine Venus and the masculine Mars, complement each other to create a very strong physical, emotional and sexual attraction. Gentle Libra may find the severity of Scorpio overwhelming, but if these two can overcome their odds, they will find that the secret to their happiness is in finding something to share which gives pleasure and satisfaction to both. Overall, Libra is tactful enough not to provoke Scorpio's sting, and there will likely be an undeniable mutual attraction between the Scales' charming, natural allure and Scorpio's smouldering, charismatic sex appeal.

Overall compatibility rating ★ 7.5 out of 10
Lucky Romance Tip ★ To attract a Scorpio, wear the colours red or burgundy, and use the crystal malachite

Libra ★ Sagittarius ♎ ♐

Libra's Air should complement Sagittarius's Fire, bringing genuine enjoyment and hours of stimulating, delightful conversation. Libra's indecisiveness, however, may bring out the Archer's more tactless side. The candid comments of the Archer can either amuse Libra greatly or puncture his cool demeanour. Either way, the Sagittarian's optimism and mental agility have the potential to be a balm for the Libran soul and food for its mind. The two of you together are bound to make an effective united front in social situations as lots of light-hearted banter is a given. Airy Libra won't stifle the free-spirited Sagittarius with impossible demands, and in turn the Sagittarius will enjoy the enlightening, stimulating and delightful company of the charming Scales. Both enjoy their freedom and independence in their own ways, and Fire complements Air perfectly in this blend. The union of your ruling planets Venus and Jupiter increases the qualities of love, happiness, success, abundance, pleasure and the overall ability to enjoy life. Although Libra needs to share things with someone exclusive and the Archer is rather non-committal, the Scales will allow for this because his Airy nature endows him with a healthy level of detachment and tolerance. Sagittarius in turn is generous enough to allow Libra to indulge in those much-loved pleasures, indulgences, luxuries and the 'good life', which he will revel in also. In living the high life however, and with their combined extravagant and indulgent tastes, these two could find their budgets - and their waistlines - stretched considerably! But aside from some minor differences, the Archer's spiritual ideals inspire Libra and the Scales can only benefit from Sagittarius's optimism, energy and buoyancy. Your energies flow together easily so long-term success is likely.

Overall compatibility rating ★ 9 out of 10
Lucky Romance Tip ★ To attract a Sagittarius, wear the colour deep purple or royal blue, and use the crystal zircon

Libra ★ Capricorn ♎ ♑

This is quite a challenging match, but once you learn to enjoy your differences, you may find each other surprisingly delightful company. The Scales' wit, elegance, grace, charm and eloquence will win the sensuous Goat over, but Capricorn's Earthy practicalities aren't always compatible with Libra's intellectual idealism. Libra's Venusian nature, with its liberal softness and love of pleasure, meets a rather cold, hard rock in Capricorn. The Goat's stern control of emotions and behaviour can turn the loving, gregarious Libran off. This is not the most workable of combinations, as hard-working Capricorn may view Libra's breezy socialising as trivial and lazy. There is generally not enough common ground here for real rapport to grow, and as Air does not mix easily with Earth, it may be hard to bridge any gaps between you. If Libra can learn to live with the Goat's natural reserve, he will be rewarded with someone who is loyal, protects, and makes effective decisions about their love and life. Indeed, the Scales can't handle the practical details of life and will either avoid them at all costs, or hand them over to someone who can - which in this case is the Goat. Libra craves affection and sharing, and Capricorn doesn't wear her heart on her sleeve, nor does she demonstrate love or warmth easily, so Libra could be left feeling neglected and unloved. Carefree Libra enjoys self-indulgence, ease and luxury, whereas frugal Capricorn takes life very seriously, thrives on responsibility and duty, and can cope with austerity a lot better than soppy, soft Libra can. If this partnership is to work, the Goat would do well to remember that the sharing of love, affection and beautiful experiences is as necessary to Libra as breathing air. Capricorn will frown upon Libra's frivolous handling of money and flirtatious behaviour, even if it is directed at *her*. Further, the Goat likes to take things slowly, steadily and cautiously, while the much more impressionable and easy going Libra will fall for a romantic trick every time. If Libra takes the time to see behind the aloof façade of the cool Capricorn, it could be well worth his while, because he will find there a sensuous, devoted, caring partner in the Goat. But Libra is often too busy whirling and whizzing around his social circle to delve deeper than what can be seen at face value.

Overall compatibility rating ★ 6 out of 10
Lucky Romance Tip ★ To attract a Capricorn, wear the colours brown or black, and use the crystal garnet

Libra ★ Aquarius ♎ ♒

As two Air signs together, you can be warm playmates or emotional tornadoes. The sceptic hidden beneath the Libran good cheer often doubts those lofty Aquarian ideals. But Air harmonises with Air, and these two also have the potential to have an intense and explosive meeting of the minds. Since these two signs are naturally friendly and need the company of others, they can share these pleasures together. However, Libra is the epitome of the personal lover, while Aquarius is the archetypal Universal lover who prefers to share interests and affections with many people. Libra's emphasis on close intimate relationships can also cause tension, as Aquarius needs to feel free and unencumbered by emotional ties. While Aquarius is largely aloof, eccentric and unpredictable, Libra uses diplomacy, grace and tact to handle things. Neither will make impossible demands on the other, as both are intellectually-based rather than feeling, smothering types, but this relationship can only work if Libra allows Aquarius freedom and does not demand too much 'together' time. Their intellectual rapport alone, however, suggests deep potential here, and can take their relationship to great heights.

Overall compatibility rating ★ 8.5 out of 10
Lucky Romance Tip ★ To attract an Aquarian, wear the colours electric blue or turquoise, and use the crystal aquamarine

Libra ★ Pisces ♎ ♓

While Pisces is driven by emotion, Libra is driven by logic. However, Libra's ruling planet Venus complements the Fish's Neptune and this should smooth any ripples. And while Water and Air don't tend to blend easily, this is the exception rather than rule in this coupling. Both are naturally romantic, tender, affectionate, and have a fond appreciation of art and beauty. The harmony between your two ruling planets, Neptune and Venus, helps to bridge the gap between your differing elements, so although you may have essentially different natures, there is potential for great affinity and rapport between you. You both enjoy and seek harmony, gentleness, love, togetherness and the magic of intimacy and sharing. You also both have a need and love of peace. Libra's innate sense of good judgement and balance will help to counteract Pisces's tendency towards confusion, escapism and impracticality. Conflicts may arise over your differing emotional qualities; Pisces feels deeply and sensitively, while Libra tends to 'feel' with the intellect, and rationalises love. To Pisces, love is intangible and ethereal, whereas Libra has no trouble articulating what he thinks of the subject. Further, the Fish's Watery depths may intrigue the Scales, but Libra will soon lose interest if the mental rapport slips beneath the surface. Libra needs to be in a relationship like he needs to breathe air, while the Fish doesn't actively seek out a soul mate and is quite content to swim solo, enjoying serendipitous moments and romantic encounters along the journey; both, however, will easily climb aboard the magical carpet of love if it presents itself, and enjoy an entrancing ride across the galaxy. If these two can overcome their different elementary emotional natures, they have the potential to be a beautiful and successful match.

Overall compatibility rating ★ 8 out of 10
Lucky Romance Tip ★ To attract a Pisces, wear the colours mauve or sea green, and use the crystal amethyst

YOUR TAROT CARDS ★ FOR LUCK, MAGIC, ENERGY, ABUNDANCE, QUESTING & MEANING
JUSTICE, THE EMPRESS & THE FOOL

Tarot and astrology are inextricably linked. All the cards of the Major Arcana, which comprises 22 of the Tarot's 78 cards, are 'ruled by' or connected with either one of the twelve zodiac signs, the planets and luminaries, or one of the four elements.

The 22 Major Arcana cards contain the richest symbolism of all the cards in the Tarot deck, each carrying a myriad of messages for the reader to decipher. The symbolism contained within these images represents the archetypal aspects of your character. It also describes the path your soul takes through each stage of life, revealing clues through which you can explore different parts of yourself. Each of the cards also represents an aspect of Universal human experience and has a name that either directly conveys the meaning of the card, such as Strength or Justice, or depicts individuals that represent these human archetypes, such as the Hermit or the Empress. The illustrations on each card contain one or more figures and tuning into a card's imagery enables you to grasp its meaning intuitively. Consider the demeanour of the characters, whether it is day or night, the background, any symbols, the buildings, the colours, the vegetation, the weather and the season. Every card has its own story to impart, and through entering that story you can gain deeper insights into the full picture of your journey so far, as well as illuminating your path ahead.

I have outlined three cards here for your sign: Justice, The Empress and The Fool, all of which have links to your zodiac sign itself Libra, your ruling planet Venus, and your element of Air. All three cards will have special meaning for your sign, and can carry powerful messages and lessons for you to reflect upon.

★ JUSTICE ★
Ruled by Libra

Keywords ★ Fairness, Morality, Balance

★ KEY THEMES ★
Karma ★ Rational Thought ★ Impartial Judgement ★ Fairness ★ Equilibrium of Mind ★ Fair and Just Decisions ★ Standing up for Beliefs ★ Doing What is Right ★ Resisting Injustice ★ Issuing or Accepting an Apology ★ Righteousness ★ Morality ★ Legal Decision or Intervention ★ Resolution ★ Balance

Number ★ 11 (or 8 in some decks)
Astrological Sign ★ Libra

THE MESSAGE ★ Some aspects of life might seem beyond our control, but at the same time, justice *does* prevail. The Justice card is about learning our lessons, being rewarded for the good we do, and likewise, being punished for any evil we do. Justice teaches us to discriminate, to make impersonal decisions and dispassionate evaluations, to weigh up, to balance, and then ultimately to make rational choices. Although the laws of nature are difficult, if not impossible, to tame and manipulate for all the human striving of fairness, justice is nevertheless one of the most noble conceptions of the human spirit. Justice represents the laws of nature, as well as the relentless workings of fate - through the slow, regular turning of the Wheel of Karma. Modern Hopi Indians believe that, in both the natural and the supernatural worlds, there is a fixed order and life is cyclical. Like the ancient Egyptians, they understand that we must remain in harmony with this Universal order and maintain our connection with it through blessings and rituals. If harmony does not prevail, then life will not progress smoothly and humanity will not prosper. Errors must be recognised and order must be restored in order for karmic forces to adjust to and overcome any adverse conditions. This is Justice's task - to maintain and restore order and equilibrium, therefore ensuring karmic balance. Justice guides you towards wise and carefully considered decisions, ones made with fairness and objectivity. It suggests that you have a decision to make, and also that a decision has been or will be made in your favour; so if you are currently in a legal dispute, it will turn out positively for you. The Justice card also solemnly reminds you to thoroughly review any legal documents or contracts before signing them.

THE STORY ★ Justice is one of the three virtues in the Tarot's Major Arcana - the others are Strength and Temperance. A very favourable card, it indicates that the outcome of the situation in question will be good, and that the querent is in a strong position to reach the correct decision over a current challenge. Justice is a detached, but fair, mediator who helps to resolve inner and outer conflicts through the courage of her convictions. The crowned figure of Justice is often seated between pillars representing mercy and punishment. In her hands she holds the balance and sword. Her face is resolute and firm in conviction and she wears no blindfold, so she sees all the facts.

THE AWAKENING ★ Justice holds the scales. Behind her throne there are sometimes depicted two upright columns representing moral strength and integrity, mercy and punishment, and she has the power to differentiate between right and wrong. She always implies the need to find or recover a balance between opposing forces or contradictory elements. She advises that although the *human* judicial system may be fooled, Divine justice can never be escaped. When Justice appears in a reading, you are coming to consciousness about your place in the Universal scheme of things. There is some way you can feel karma working in your life. Maybe you are winning a custody or law suit case, or perhaps you have a newfound sense of yourself as powerful and moving through life with purpose. Maybe some conflict in your life has come to a resolution, or things have worked out after a period of imbalance. Whatever the case, things are setting themselves right again and you can feel your own peace returning. You understand that what is happening is a result of past actions that are having karmic results. But you also have to realise that even if things aren't working out so well, or if you are off-balance, that nature works in calm, quiet ways, sometimes giving us what we *need* rather than what we *want*.

THE LESSON ★ The Justice card belongs to Libra, the cardinal Air sign of social fairness and equality, symbolised by the Scales. Libra, being ruled by Venus (goddess of love) considers everything in terms of others. Libra loves beauty and harmony, and wants to bring her surroundings to a state of peaceful co-existence. In this way, Libra is Nemesis, the cords of retribution and just rewards, that draw the human race together, and urges to connect each of us with the All - after all, a blessing on one of Earth's children blesses all, just as a curse on one hurts all. Justice advises to be practical, rigorous, stern but fair, kind, patient, objective, honest, and sympathetic to those weaker than yourself. Of course, it is always possible to appeal against what has been judged. But, once the sword has fallen, a page has been turned.

SYMBOLISM *★ In the Tarot, Justice is always shown as a woman, following the tradition of the ancient Greeks for whom Themis was the goddess of justice. She wears the red robe of worldly power, her sword ready to cut through any ignorance that might impede her from reaching spiritual enlightenment, while her scales help her to weigh up the value of all things and maintain a fair balance.

On one of the throne's shorter pillars often sits an owl, the ancient bird of wisdom, known for its clear vision and ability to see in the dark. Colour is an important element of this card. Red, the colour of passion and desire, and green, healing and love, work together to create harmony. The colour purple, which symbolises wisdom, is also often used, as wise insights are necessary in order to make sound judgements. The imagery in this card suggests the theme of mental clarity, and the need for the mind to seek logical solutions to difficult problems.

The Justice card counsels us to be aware of the consequences of our actions, that we control our own destiny, and to behave responsibly and with dignity. It signifies the wisdom to take responsibility for the way we live our lives and brings the understanding that there are underlying cosmic laws by which we are all affected; it therefore symbolises the realisation that whatever events occur in your life, you have a choice in how you respond to them, which will then determine your attitudes, perceptions and directions thereafter.

At the heart of the Justice card are the notions of self-understanding and the idea that you control your own fate and are thus accountable for all your actions.

The goddess on the Justice card holds the scales to weigh up right against wrong, and the sword to enforce her judgement. She stands as if ready for action and wears items of armour, symbolising a determination to fight for what she knows is right. Sometimes the scales may be gold and silver, symbolising the integration of feeling and logic.

When the Justice card appears, it indicates firstly that events have turned out the way they were 'meant' to work out; that is, situations happening to you now have been shaped by your past actions and decisions. In other words, you have what you justly deserve. Secondly, it indicates a possibility and a need for seeing the truth of this outcome, signifying absolute honesty - with your past and yourself. At the same time, it shows the possibility that your actions in the future can be changed by a lesson learned in your present situation. Look for the seed of truth in your current situation, and it can guide you to make the most accordant decisions leading to your optimal future self. This card represents seeing all the facts, without succumbing to temptation or envy to misguide you. The Justice card suggests the ignorance of the law is no more excuse in the courts of life than in the courts of people. It tells us that laws must be studied and obeyed if the penalties and punishment for rebelling are to be avoided. However, being too harsh is also not ideal and the balance must not be tipped. Ultimately, Justice carries the message that, although the human judicial system can be fooled and flawed, Divine 'higher' justice can never be escaped.

Librans are recommended to carry one of these cards with them to illumine their paths, and to magnetise that for which they are asking. Go forth and claim the magic which is yours by using the symbolism of Justice as your guide!

★ THE EMPRESS ★
Ruled by Venus

Keywords ★ Nurturance, Fertility, Security

★ KEY THEMES ★
Creation ★ Fertility ★ Emotional Wealth ★ Motherhood ★ Happy, Stable Relationships ★ Growth ★ Lavish Abundance ★ Birthing and Fostering Dreams ★ Art ★ Creativity ★ Affinity with Nature ★ Security ★ Pleasure ★ Harmony ★ Material Comforts ★ Fruitfulness ★ Ripeness ★ Mother ★ Wife

Number ★ 3
Astrological Signs ★ Taurus & Libra

THE MESSAGE ★ The Empress can be linked to the Full Moon, which, upon reaching its shining bright potential, must slowly fade into the darkness and become a mere sliver. This Earthly mother teaches about the wisdom of nature, its rhythms and cycles of growth, death and rebirth, and the idea that these cycles are present within all humans. She also imparts knowledge about women and their ways and needs, leading by example. The Empress, the archetypal fertile Earth Mother, can help bring daydreams to fruition in a world where logic and intuition should dwell together as heaven and Earth do. As such, the Empress is telling you to give birth to your dreams, to nurture yourself and others, spend time in nature, and indulge in creative and artistic endeavours. She suggests a possible pregnancy, a harmonious home environment and progress with your plans. She encourages you to enjoy material comforts and sexual fulfilment but to be wary of overindulgence. Enjoy the beautiful things in life, knowing that you deserve to be exquisitely and Divinely provided for.

THE STORY ★ The Empress represents the Great Mother, pure and simple. She promises abundance, birth, growth, harmony, community, and relationship. She can represent the Earth from which all life is born, and to which it returns at the end of its cycle. The first Empress-type statues were the small pregnant 'Venus' figurines from the Ice Age in Europe and Russia (at least 30,000 BC). These tiny goddess figures are pregnant to bursting point and generally without distinctive features of face, hands or feet - the emphasis clearly lay upon their full breasts and bellies. Much feminine wisdom has faded with the rise of patriarchal societies in our modern lives, but we still hold the basis for these mysteries within our bodies. The Empress in her contemporary 'seductress' pose symbolises the unconscious knowledge modern women share of the ancient mysteries and female reverence, of healing and transformation, that live on in our much-diminished but ever-pure Divinity. The Empress feels her connection to the Earth. She knows - has always known - the mystery of procreation, the potential for growing and nurturing life, the sacred act of birthing, and the communal life close to the soil - a time when people did not make war, but spent their leisure time making love and art. The Empress is a sensual, practical woman who appreciates good, wholesome, hearty food, nature and a simple life. She is nurturing and generous, and teaches that you need to foster dreams and desires. If the card preceding this, the High Priestess, holds the secrets of life, then the Empress is what gives that life soul and emotion, for she represents the understanding and the power of that life. The Empress's power lies primarily in feelings, as she is able to exploit both the riches of the heart and the psyche.

THE LESSON ★ This is a warmly emotional card, suggesting love, luxury and comfort. The Empress brings out your artistic side, opens your love of beauty, and heightens your aesthetic appreciation. The Empress represents 'prosperity thinking' and the power of positive imagination. The Empress is a materially and practically inclined card rather than psychically- or spiritually-oriented, although she does have links with the Divine feminine. Your hopes *will* come to fruition, finances *will* improve, green leaves *will* sprout, examples and symbols of fertility *will* abound, and you *will* begin to feel more confident as you reap the rewards of your efforts. And indeed, ask the Great Mother for what you need. Remember, Venus (Ishtar-Aphrodite) is the wishing star.

SYMBOLISM * ★ The Empress is the third numbered card in the Major Arcana. The number three is indicative of synthesis and harmony, childbirth and maternal productivity. The Empress is shown as an Earth Mother, gentle and caring, surrounded by comfort and plenitude. Her crown is surmounted by twelve stars representing the signs of the zodiac. The Empress, as the Earth Mother, sometimes appears in a field of corn, symbolising her link with nature. She has a strong connection with motherhood and is portrayed as pregnant, or at least wearing a flowing outfit which hints at it. She has been called 'the star-crowned empress, herself the morning star'. This is a direct identification with the goddess Venus, otherwise known as 'the morning star', who, as well as her famed associations with love, is also a deity connected with fruitfulness and harvest.

Still other cards depict a beautiful, serene woman with long, flowing fair hair that resembles the golden fields of corn, dotted with poppies, surrounding her. A waterfall and forest can be seen beyond the rich fields, and at her feet a horn of plenty overflows with fruit, symbolising the Earth's abundant bounty. The Empress is a symbol of potential possibly fulfilled by the hint of pregnancy that her loose and flowing robe suggests. Her robe is adorned with seeded-pomegranates, her lap contains a sheaf of corn, and she wears a necklace of ten pearls, symbolising the ten planets that comprise the Solar system. The twelve stars in her crown represent the twelve months of the year, the twelve signs of the zodiac, and the twelve hours each of day and night; she wears a necklace with four stones, standing for the four seasons of life: birth, blossom, fruition and decay; indeed, all these life stages and processes are presided over by the Empress, and this imagery points to natural cycles, growth, abundance, fertility, and the ever-present possibilities of new life.

The left hand of the Empress points towards the sky and the heavens. Her right hand holds a spectre pointing to the ground, symbolising her anchorage to the Earth. She also holds a protective shield with the symbol of an eagle, and is normally depicted in natural surroundings with a stream flowing behind her. The position of her hands connects her with the Magician card and shows that she is the primal creative force, representing motherhood and security, in a way that ultimately brings together heaven and Earth.

The Empress nurtures and nourishes, representing any process that involves physical growth and sustenance. She represents a time of passion, a period during which we approach life through feelings and pleasure rather than thought and ideas. This passion can be either sexual or motherly; either way, it is deeply experienced. Marriage, children, and issues involving motherhood and creativity will be positively affected when this card shows up.

The Empress reveals that it is time for birth, whether literal or creative. Whatever has been gestating in the previous card, The High Priestess, is now ready to be born. When she appears in a spread, she denotes a time of growth, of flourishing crops, creative ideas and all things reaching their full maturity.

Ultimately, the Empress represents happy, stable relationships, growth and fertility. This card is a symbol of fulfilled potential, creative pursuits, the satisfaction of nurturing something to fruition (as well as the pain of its loss), and symbolises love, marriage and motherhood. Its divinatory meanings are feminine progress, fruitfulness, pregnancy, security, mother, sister, wife, marriage, children, feminine influence, practicality, accomplishment, nurturing, and the ability to gently motivate others.

★ THE FOOL ★
Ruled by Uranus & the Element of Air

Keywords ★ Beginnings, Innocence, Exploration

"Trusting Your Inner Elf"

★ KEY THEMES ★
Fresh Beginnings ★ Adventure ★ Quest ★ Excitement ★ Asserting Your Independence ★ Creative Solutions ★ Spontaneity ★ Egolessness ★ Innocence ★ The Need for Optimism ★ Naiveté ★ Unexpected Opportunities ★ Courage ★ Folly ★ Happy-Go-Lucky Mortal, About to Step Off a Cliff into the Abyss ★ Impulse

Meditation ★ "I have the courage to step forward; I am not afraid of the unknown."

Number ★ Zero (or 22 in some decks)
Astrological Signs ★ Aquarius, Gemini, Libra & Aries

THE STORY ★ The Fool card symbolises the state of potential from which all possibilities arise. It is the purest embodiment of the self on the quest for spiritual awakening. When the Fool appears in a Tarot spread, it suggests that you are about to embark on a journey that will fundamentally change you - either literally or by changing your outlook on life.

You may not be certain of what lies ahead, but you must be willing to take the chance.

THE STORY ★ The Fool is a foolish man. And as such, he knows everything, but is unaware that he does. Or, he possesses all the gifts, all the truths, all the wisdom, all the joys, all the wonders of the seen and unseen worlds, but is totally unaware of it. He must therefore submit himself to the various trials of life to develop his faculties and become an enlightened being. The Fool represents the Self on a journey, who grows and learns with each new encounter. Wide-eyed and innocent as a newborn child, The Fool has descended from the celestial realms, eager to begin his mystical journey on the path towards enlightenment. All is new to him and he has not yet learned to fear. Living from moment to moment, going forward without plan nor care, unaware of potential perils and joyful, in his luggage he carries the memories, instincts and experiences of past lives, waiting to be utilised this time around. He carries a wand symbolising the pure faith of his actions, upon which sits a head that looks backwards, representing The Fool's past as he moves ever-forward. The dog leaping and bounding behind him symbolises the purity of the animal nature of our physical bodies and is seen in playful harmony with The Fool. The backdrop is suffused with green, the colour of growth, and the sky is filled with the fresh light of a spring season, signalling shining, new life. Like the court jesters who maintained his tradition, The Fool is truthful, and has no contaminating malice or desires.

SYMBOLISM *★ This card depicts the Fool wandering off, his few possessions slung over his shoulder in a small bag hung from a pilgrim's staff, oblivious to the chasm ahead, with his dog jumping at his leg. Symbolically, his bag carries his experiences. He does not abandon them, for he is not thoughtless, they simply do not control him in the way that *our* traumas or memories so often control our lives. The stick upon which his bag casually hangs, is, in some interpretations, actually a wand, a symbol of power and magic. The Fool card's image symbolises the instinctive life force that both holds him back and urges him on. Like its ruler Uranus, the Fool is the spirit of chaos, of the unexpected, but also about innocence and the simple joys of living. This card belongs anywhere in the deck, in combination with and between any of the other cards, offering an animating force to more static images and symbols. As such, he assists during times of transition, and also in times of difficult passage.

The Fool's staff represents the Suit of Wands, symbolic of passionate, fiery energy. He grasps the staff firmly, as he does all of life's opportunities, and although it is a symbol of power, the Fool uses it in a playful manner.

The Fool's cloak is usually blue, representing his inner search for wisdom and truth. And when he finds his enlightenment, he will be eager to communicate it to others.

The Fool is usually the first card in the Tarot deck, the starting point of the Tarot 'experience'. In some early decks he appeared at the end of the Major Arcana rather than at the beginning, as he not only begins our journey but may also accompany us throughout it - this is essentially because he symbolises our very self. When he first sets out at the beginning of his path, he is a stranger to his inner self and lives primarily in his conscious mind, but by the end of his journey he has glimpsed the deeper mysteries of his real self. The Fool seeks the truth, and turns his attention towards the spirit in search of it. There is in the Fool an element of the Divine trickster, and even though the Fool doesn't know what he is doing in the sense of logical thought, he moves from an impulse that arises out of the infinite possibilities emanating from the state represented by the number 'zero'. The Fool is simple, innocent, trusting and ignorant of the potential trials, setbacks and pitfalls that await him, and he is prepared to abandon his old ways and follow his quest by taking a leap into the unknown. Indeed, the Fool represents the need to let go of old ways and begin something new, untested and unexperienced. For those willing to follow the Fool's example and deviate from the path society has set out for us, this leap can bring joy, adventure, and finally, for those with the courage to continue even when the path becomes fearsome, the leap will bring peace, knowledge and liberation.

Containing all possibilities, the Fool represents the phenomenon of synchronicity or coincidences between happenings, and is the part of us that unconsciously connects to the greater Universal whole, so things are constantly happening to us that involve the unspoken and often unacknowledged links between our thoughts and the events outside of ourselves. If you are open to magic, you will accept these synchronicities on an intellectual level, and in turn will notice such events more frequently and learn to appreciate them more fully.

This card can be said to represent the human soul that is unselfconsciously happy to be alive, that does not yet reflect back upon itself, the spark of life that reincarnates again and again until it truly awakens to itself. Reincarnation is the secret key to the Fool, and the Fool is indeed the 'secret' key, or at least significantly the first door which opens us up to the rest of the Tarot experience. The Fool, whose awareness is limited to the present moment, moves from moment to moment, life to life, without intellectual consideration or care for what has gone before and what will be in the future. Representing innocence, the Fool is perpetually young and always starting afresh. He believes in himself and instinctively trusts his body and the general flow of life.

Astrologically, the Fool is ruled by the Air element, making it as free as the wind. Uranus, considered the most eccentric of the planets, gives the card's symbolism qualities of intellectual brilliance, intuitive flashes, lawlessness, reform, inventiveness and originality. Linked to this rebellious planet, it also promises mystery, a dash of genius, adventure, and a great opportunity to reinvent your life. It impels you to listen to your own inner guidance about following your dreams while still staying open to outside guidance and information; actively seek any insight you may need for your leap.

Although some divinatory meanings of this card are thoughtlessness, insecurity, folly, apathy, frivolity, extravagance, lack of discipline, immaturity, irrationality, hesitation, indecision, delirium, frenzy, enthusiasm and naivety, it also proclaims that nothing can harm you, whatever you do, so take a risk! It does, however, advise to look before you leap - a measured, calculated risk will reap the greatest rewards - and lessons. This card symbolises new beginnings in all senses, courageous leaps into some new phase of life, and is a particularly potent symbol when that jump is taken from some inner prompting and deep feeling rather than careful planning.

Not limited by ordinary social conventions and uncomplicated and unanalytical by nature, the Fool is never afraid to believe in something Divine or greater than ego. Naturally flowing, trusting, naïve and spontaneous, the Fool often plunges into the cosmic experience without fear or expectation. And indeed, it is the Fool in each of us which urges us away from lethargy and towards enlightenment and transformation without fear of the future. And along your travels, it is also worth noting and reminding yourself that even a fool can have flashes of great wisdom and sudden lightning bolt thoughts, reminiscent of the brilliant but ever-unpredictable Uranus, ruler of your fellow Air sign Aquarius.

* Please note that the images described are not found in all Tarot decks. The images in different decks can differ considerably.

THE TAROT'S SUIT OF SWORDS ★ REPRESENTING THE AIR ELEMENT

The Swords correspond with the Air element and are an especially interesting and meaningful metaphor. Swords, or the mind, organise by dividing, and quite literally cutting through things. Being of the Air element, the Swords are associated with ideas, the intellect, mental activity, thought processes, and mental insights, attitudes and clarity. Air cannot be seen, gripped, grasped or commanded of, and can only be felt with subtle 'other' senses - the higher mind being one of them. We know the air is there through its apparent physical presence such as wisps of wind, but we cannot see it, touch it or even embrace it. In this way, the Swords suit can signify a certain elusiveness, something that can somehow evade us. But it is nonetheless a powerful force. With the Air suit, illusions are recognised and shattered in the pursuit of the inner kernel of truth, knowledge and wisdom that the Swords embody - but the quest is fraught with painful lessons and is not always easy. These challenges will lead to greater understanding.

The story of Swords begins with the core connection to the all-wise, all-seeing eye of the spirit. This Divine essence first manifests itself in the mind and then those thoughts create form. Everything you see results from an initial thought that was put into action. As well as relating to the conscious direction of the intellect and will, the Swords also reveal hidden motivations and attitudes that can influence a situation. Cards from this suit advise us to either go to the core of the problem or to cut ourselves free in order to start afresh. Considered to be powerful and potentially destructive and dangerous, the Tarot Swords can indicate battles and enemies, but they can also be used constructively, to summon courage and a more conscious and astute quality of mind. Even though they have long had a reputation as harbingers of unhappiness and discomfort, this suit still serves a useful purpose. Without the ability to use reason and logic we risk being constantly swept away by our emotions, with all the potential for disaster that this could bring. The Swords can therefore assist in bringing about increased clarity and foresight, which we can use to avert trouble that may be brewing, and nip explosiveness in the bud. The Swords may be connected with hostility, sorrows, loss, struggle, action, change, bitterness, power, oppression, malice and conflict, but they are also associated with fortitude, decisiveness, audacity, tact, fairness, strength, bravery, ambition, force and truth, as well as with ideas and communication. Swords are almost always double-edged, which symbolises the fine balance that is needed between the intellect and power, and how these two forces can be used for good or evil. Overall, the Suit of Swords reveals our state of mind and how we use its mighty force. In a deck of playing cards, Swords correspond to Spades.

THE LUCKY 13 ★ LIBRAN TIPS FOR INCREASED MAGIC, LUCK & MAGNETISM

1 ★ Incorporate Libran symbols into your daily life to remind yourself of your soul's mission.

2 ★ Use the crystal Opal in any form in your daily life - wear it, meditate with it, hold it and carry it with you everywhere! Opal is said to improve vitality by magnifying energy, enhance one's self-image, improve one's fortune or luck, have protective powers, and stimulate cosmic consciousness. Absorbent and reflective, on a spiritual level it picks up thoughts and feelings, amplifies them, and returns them to source. A protective and karmic stone, it teaches that what you put out comes back. An excellent aid for transformation, opal promotes self-worth and helps you understand your full potential, inducing states of emotion and well-being which can assist in attracting wonderful things to you.

3 ★ Wear or surround yourself with the colours rose pink, light blue and green.

4 ★ Learn the way of the Ram by learning to cultivate greater independence, a heightened self-awareness, decisiveness, and more initiative. Aries has much to teach the Libran soul. Rise to the challenge … Be brave and bold and plunge right in … Focus on building your self-confidence … Care less what others think of you … Get off the fence and make that decision ... Fight for what you believe in ... Feel the wonders of the flames lapping at your feet - or better still, develop the strength of mind to walk over hot coals ... Take a risk ... Speak your mind and become more assertive ... Be raw, spontaneous and edgy - beauty is deeper than the skin - be courageous enough to go deeper! ... Dance as if no one's watching ... Jump from the frying pan into the Fire ... it's *all* within you!

5 ★ Use your lucky number 6 whenever you are needing an extra stroke of luck.

6 ★ Magnify and celebrate your relating and affectionate nature, your sense of beauty and balance, your ethereal spirituality, and your dignity, grace and elegance.

7 ★ Remind yourself of your quest constantly, that is by speaking, breathing and *truly living* your dreams and insights - give them form beyond simply sitting on the fence and daydreaming about them!

8 ★ Focus your energies on exploring your ego-self, and transforming yourself through developing a stronger sense of *you*, that doesn't rely on others for validation or to get by. Connect with your natural charm and eloquence to get what you want through any means possible.

9 ★ Use your innate powers of balance, justice, fairness and love to attune yourself to the metaphysical realm, and to draw that which you

desire towards you. If you can develop simple faith in the positive outcome of events, you can easily use your Airy intuition to great creative effect.

10 ★ Tap into and utilise your ability to relate, understand, empathise with, and transform others through sharing your emotions, spirit and soul. But to do that, you'll need to ease yourself gently out of your warm and fuzzy comfort zone and into a clearer reality.

11 ★ View your fair and impartial nature as a strength and call forth the powers of your delightful, gifted, unique self. Be who you *really* are, without reservation or apology, and the rest will fall into place.

12 ★ Become the 'Gracious Social Equaliser' of others - and yourself - that you were born to be!

13 ★ Once you have mastered purer focus, decisiveness, assertiveness, and a stronger sense of your individual self, learn to share the resulting abundance, insights and knowledge with others so they too can walk the Higher Path!

HAVE YOU PACKED YOUR MAGICAL BAG FOR THE JOURNEY?

If you wish to increase and draw more luck, love and abundance into your life, a power pack is essential. For Librans, I would recommend carrying or wearing the following items on you on your travels. Then just sit back and watch as magic pours into your experiences and realities, both inner and outer!

★ One of each of the following gemstones: Opal, Tourmaline, Sapphire, Jade, Rose Quartz, Diamond
★ Tarot cards Justice and The Empress (and The Fool card too, if you wish)
★ A raven in any form (use your imagination!)
★ Something made of copper
★ A scales symbol in any form
★ A postcard or image from a tropical place (representing your Sanguine disposition). Bon Voyage!
★ A postcard from the future to yourself, proclaiming, 'Wish You Were Here!'

A FINAL WORD ★ TAPPING INTO THE MAGIC OF LIBRA

There is something inherently magical about Libra, the fair, balanced Scales. Nothing is distasteful about you. You are blessed with a courteous, polished, tolerant, generous, sophisticated and thoughtful character, and use it to your advantage through your relationships. Civilised and refined, you seem to have a sixth sense about what is appropriate and not appropriate, and indeed, what is required of you, in social interactions, which adds to your considerable charm. In fact, it was probably a Libran who wrote the book on etiquette, social behaviour and manners. In your search for truth, beauty, justice and harmony, you will keep these in the forefront of your mind when engaging with anyone or embarking upon anything.

The cosmos has endowed Librans with the precious and important gifts of grace, elegance, charm, wit, sociability, and the ability to swim deftly through society because your people skills are so impressive. Whether you are fully cognisant of it or not, a magical reservoir of energy is available to you to tap into whenever it is needed.

Finally, to attune yourself to luck, harmony and success, Librans should wear, eat, inhale, meditate upon, create, design, and dance with any or all of the suggested luck-enhancers for your Sun sign to receive the most beneficial astral vibrations these 'boosters' can offer you. Wearing, decorating and working with the amazing powers of all your lucky guides, animals, crystals, colours, woods, cards, herbs, foods, places, talismans, planetary influences, charms, numbers, and other magical tips contained within the words of this very book, will bring you greater abundance, love, magic, energy, happiness and personal power, and attract all manner of things to you like bees to sweet flowers. This, my Libran friends, I promise you - and Aquarians *never* lie.

Good luck on the rest of your amazing life journey, and may the LUCK be with you!

Lani is also available for personal Astrology, Numerology, Aura * & Tarot reading consultations, via post, email, Skype and in-person.
Please email lalana76@bigpond.com for more information.

In-person only

Facebook Page ★ Astrology Magic

Other Books in the **Lucky Astrology** Series

Lucky Astrology ★ Aries
Lucky Astrology ★ Taurus
Lucky Astrology ★ Gemini
Lucky Astrology ★ Cancer
Lucky Astrology ★ Leo
Lucky Astrology ★ Virgo
Lucky Astrology ★ Scorpio
Lucky Astrology ★ Sagittarius
Lucky Astrology ★ Capricorn
Lucky Astrology ★ Aquarius
Lucky Astrology ★ Pisces

Order your copies now, from White Light Publishing House, at www.whitelightpublishingau.com

www.ingramcontent.com/pod-product-compliance
Lightning Source LLC
Chambersburg PA
CBHW071157300426
44113CB00009B/1232